"What an exemplary book by an amazing scholar who is also—at the very same time—an incredible parent, a spiritually centered person, *and* an activist for earth care and social justice. T. Wilson Dickinson tackles head-on an angst that plagues every parent today—what does it mean to bring children into a world of climate catastrophes? His answer joins sage discernment about life priorities with concrete wisdom for daily living, giving readers a wealth of insight, encouragement, and hope."

—Bonnie J. Miller-McLemore
Professor emerita of religion, psychology, and culture, Vanderbilt University

"In this book, T. Wilson Dickinson holds not only his son's hand but ours too. With the richness of the Psalms, he guides us now and into the future through times unknown and spaces growing in loss and destruction. This book is like the mask we hear about in the airplanes. We put it first on ourselves, so we are able to help our kids. Dickinson teaches us to read the Psalms and offer healing to the world."

—Cláudio Carvalhaes
Professor of worship, Union Theological Seminary

"This is a deeply learned and intimate book that seamlessly integrates elements of personal memoir, theological and biblical exposition, critical analysis, parenting wisdom, and social change theory. T. Wilson Dickinson is the rare author who can draw from so many complex streams of thought and lived experience to speak plainly and insightfully about what it means to be fully and faithfully human at this fraught time in history. As a father as well, I was moved and inspired. This book should be widely read, discussed, and shared."

—Timothy Reinhold Eberhart
Associate professor of ecological theology and practice,
Garrett-Evangelical Theological Seminary

"T. Wilson Dickinson's beautiful reflections on the Psalms may break your heart open, but will heal it as well. His love for his son stunningly translates for the love all of us have for our sons and daughters, and our hopes that they may live a healthy and spirited future in a world full of challenges. He has done all of us a great service as a father, a poetic writer, and a man of faith."

—Gary Paul Nabhan
Author of *Jesus for Farmers and Fishers*

Singing *the* Psalms *with* My Son

Singing *the* Psalms *with* My Son

Praying and Parenting for a Healed Planet

T. Wilson Dickinson

CASCADE *Books* • Eugene, Oregon

SINGING THE PSALMS WITH MY SON
Praying and Parenting for a Healed Planet

Cascade Books
An Imprint of Wipf and Stock Publishers
199 W. 8th Ave., Suite 3
Eugene, OR 97401

www.wipfandstock.com

PAPERBACK ISBN: 978-1-6667-4393-7
HARDCOVER ISBN: 978-1-6667-4394-4
EBOOK ISBN: 978-1-6667-4395-1

Cataloguing-in-Publication data:

Names: Dickinson, T. Wilson, author.
Title: Singing the Psalms with my son : praying and parenting for a healed planet / T. Wilson Dickinson.
Description: Eugene, OR: Cascade Books, 2023 | Includes bibliographical references and index.
Identifiers: ISBN 978-1-6667-4393-7 (paperback) | ISBN 978-1-6667-4394-4 (hardcover) | ISBN 978-1-6667-4395-1 (ebook)
Subjects: LCSH: Bible. Psalms—Criticism, interpretation, etc. | Ecotheology.
Classification: BS1430.52 D60 2023 (paperback) | BS1430.52 (ebook)

VERSION NUMBER 060723

To Carly and Teddy, whose love, joy,
and laughter bring healing every day.

Contents

Acknowledgments

For a book on the gifts of parenting, prayer, and the commons of creation, the opportunity to give thanks to all who made the present work possible is as welcome as it is daunting. These meditations grew out of the soil of my shared life with so many people and communities—too many to name. Anything that passes for wisdom or hope in the following pages is an echo of what I have received or participated in.

I am especially grateful to friends and communities that read over parts of this book or earlier incarnations of these meditations, and helped to guide and shape it: Bonnie Miller-McLemore, Joe Blosser, Leah Schade, Sean Gladding, the Lexington Theological Seminary faculty and staff (Loida Martell, Emily Askew, Jerry Sumney, Dolores Yilibuw, and Michael Grigoni), the Association of Disciples for Theological Discussion (especially Newell Williams, Xochitl Alvizo, Larry Bouchard, and Marti Steussy), and the Practical Theology Unit of the American Academy of Religion (especially Allison Covey, Tallessyn Zawn Grenfell-Lee, and Sabrina Muller).

I am thankful for conversations with friends and colleagues, some of which have been in ongoing dialogue about this project, others who have gifted me with a seed of an idea in a passing conversation: the Green Christians Dinner Church, the Land Working Group of the Christ Seminar (Joerg Rieger, Siobhan Garrigan, Jake Erikson, James Perkinson, and David Galston), Anna Peterson, Carol Devine, Tim Eberhart, Allyn Maxfield-Steele, Fred Bahnson, Jack Caputo, Claudio Carvalhaes, Kiara Jorgenson, Lydia Wylie-Kellermann, Sarah Spendgeman, Peter Heltzel, Avery Davis Lamb, Derrick Weston, Sarah Ogletree, Anna Woofenden, Sam Chamelin, Tripp Fuller, David Dault, Rufus Burnett, Anna Mercedes, Melanie Harris, Jeremy Porter, Jeremy Paden, Olivia Updegrove, Rebecca Barnes, Jessica Maudlin, Jerry Cappel, Catherine Duffy, Josh Davis, Andrew Wilkes, Clayton Crockett, Ward Blanton, Tim Conder, Dan Rhodes, the McBrayers, and

Acknowledgments

students from sections of my course on pastoral theology. Many thanks to Rodney Clapp and the whole team at Cascade Books for shepherding and promoting this project.

I can only begin to acknowledge and express my gratitude to my family: to everyone at Dickinson Headquarters, who allowed me to write a bit about our lives, provided the space and time to write, and who have created a community where we can all begin to imagine a different, more just and joyful life together; to my brothers Jon and Bart, for their friendship and humor; to my late dad Bart, who showed me a path of fatherhood guided by kindness, wonder, deep faith, musical joy, and patient care; to my mom Suetta and my sister Becky, who have shown me the genius and grace of unfailing care; to my wife Carly, whose companionship brings joy and whose love continually shows me the way in our partnership as parents.

Finally, to those of the next generation and still to come I acknowledge my debts and deep thanks: to Logan, for your brilliance and your passion for a brighter future; to Teddy, whose very miraculous existence has been the greatest gift of my life, and whose laughter, creativity, compassion, curiosity, intelligence, and joy have shown me another way to live. I pray that your elders may learn from you and that collectively we can find ways to meet this moment of crisis and the legacies of injustice so that we can begin the long, intergenerational work of healing—each other and the planet.

Introduction

ONE OF THE SIMPLEST joys of my life is being able to hold my six-year-old son Teddy's hand. Often I hold a little too tightly, for fear that he might wander into harm's way. On this particular morning we are on a walk and have stopped to look at a stream. For a moment I feel that the world is as it should be. The morning light glistens on the water as it rushes and almost sings. Though it is little more than a drainage ditch, a line from the Psalter pours forth from my heart and illuminates the blessing that is before me: "There is a river whose streams make glad the city of God" (Ps 46:4a). I hold my son's hand as we wander along and share in the goodness of God's creation.

Turning around to the abandoned lot we are standing on, Teddy asks, "Why isn't there a house here?" The absence of a house is conspicuous on this street. The whole street is lined with houses, except for the elementary school nearby, and its spacious front lawn. This lot is a place that I have walked by thousands of times—having lived in this neighborhood in central Kentucky for most of my life. I tell him, "There used to be a gas station here when I was your age. The tanks they kept the gas in leaked into the ground. Now nothing can be here, probably for a very long time." In an instant I am reminded that things are not as they should be. Systems of extraction and exploitation have made a mess of things.

I glance over to the lot next to this one and recall who pays most dearly for this desecration. The adjacent lot used to have a few trailers on it and the house was cut up into several apartments. I heard that the tenants never stayed for long because it smelled like gas in the house and people would get sick. A couple of years ago, the housing was condemned and the trailers were removed.

Looking back at the stream, I am reminded that this low-lying land sometimes floods. The stream runs over its banks, fills the street, and transforms nearby lawns into ponds. It floods more often than when I was young. Knotted together in this one little spot is a reminder of the damage that has been done to the earth and a harbinger of things to come as climate change intensifies.

I hold a bit more tightly to my son's hand. My heart breaks as I imagine the world that he and his generation will inherit. This seemingly cataclysmic future is too much to bear. The psalm calls back to me, singing, "God is our refuge and strength . . . though the earth should change." (Ps 46:1–2). Such a promise is not the offering of an otherworldly escape. Rather, the prayer seeks to draw our attention to "the works of the LORD" (Ps 46:8a). We are to look for a different kind of power and security than empires have often trained us to trust. The psalmist declares, God "makes wars to cease to the end of the earth / God breaks the bow and shatters the spear" (Ps 46:9a).[1] This prayer calls upon us: "Be still and know that I am God" (Ps 46:10a)!

I try to take a deep breath to still myself, to come back to my son, and to see the works of God. I notice that my son's attention has returned to the stream. He still hears only its song and sees the mosaic of divinity that the dappled light has created on its surface. What is so wonderful in holding his hand is not my desire to clamp down to protect and control. Rather, between our hands there moves the power of love and care. In this simple space a whole way of life and an entire logic is incarnated. Perhaps this is a bond strong enough to bear such fears. It could be that it is through our relationships of love that we can find a way to heal and live on in the midst of the brokenness. I realize that in this moment, I am not holding Teddy's hand—he is holding mine.

The emerging realities of climate change are terrifying. When I look upon the future with my son in my mind I am simply overwhelmed. I find myself stuttering and stammering. In such matters I am unschooled and unprepared. On the contrary, the training I have received often leads me to avoid the reality of such problems as I busy myself serving the structures that are causing the ecological crisis in the first place.

This book is an invitation to listen to the Psalms and the gifts of parenthood so that we can transform these fears into acts of hope. The prayerful poems of the Psalter can guide us step by step down paths that typically feel too dark and anxiety-provoking to even face. The Psalms speak with an emotional range that is often obscured in our air-brushed, numbed-out, and ready-made lives. Their poetic lines give voice to prayers that cry in pain, tremble in loss, strain in anger, dance with joy, sing in praise, and stand firm in hope. This pregnant poetry holds the promise of practices of prayer that may shape our hearts.

I first turned to the Psalms during the decade that my father suffered from dementia. Faced with the ambiguous loss of slowly saying goodbye to parts of my dad and our relationship, I found myself struggling to even name the pain I felt. The poetry of the Psalter gave voice to the kind of suffering that is silenced by the sanitized, stoic, and polite structures of the culture to which I belong. In the Psalms, I found prayers in which profound loss could be acknowledged and held alongside abiding hope.

When I became a father myself, the teaching and guidance of the Psalms deepened, as my anxieties turned from a past that seemed to be lost, to a frightening future.[2] The threats of climate change also mark a number of ambiguous losses—from the concrete but slow loss of habitats and entire species, to the more ephemeral losses of our trust in the structures that shape our lives and the dreams that we have for our children. The Psalms have given me prayers that articulate these fears and hopeful visions for a future that exceeded those that I once had. These prayers point us toward dreams that reach beyond individual success to collective and creational visions of a beautiful and healed world.

Like the practices of prayer offered by the Psalter, simple activities of care also offer subtle lessons and a way of wisdom. The deafening busyness of our work lives often renders these everyday and habitual aspects as mere background noise. Hiding in plain sight in the spaces of our homes are lessons that can build our capacity for curiosity, creativity, collaboration, and the pursuit of the common good.[3]

We need this full range of expression and power because climate change is rooted in all of our social, political, and economic systems. Responding faithfully to these challenges demands we engage in the long work of joining movements for justice to transform these structures. The intersectional character of the ecological crisis is often missed because these issues are typically spoken of as technical problems with technological solutions. In 2017, Project Drawdown brought together leading scientists and policy makers and crunched the numbers for the best responses to climate change that were available. They demonstrated that we already have the technology to reduce the carbon currently in the atmosphere. It would simply need to be applied and scaled up. What we lack is the social, political, and economic capacity to do so. Furthermore, most of the transformations needed are not solely technological. On Drawdown's accounting, the changes possible in the energy sector account for less than a quarter of the reductions required to begin to reduce greenhouse gases in the atmosphere. The reductions possible in this sector are significantly less than changes related to food. The same could be said for the combined sectors of land use and the empowerment of women and girls.[4] Climate change demands social change.

Whereas we often place our hopes for change in the centers of power, we would do well to also turn our energies to the relationships that surround us. There is a place in between unthinkably large systems and lone individuals. On this level there are households, communities, networks, and movements. So long as we continue to try to face down these large systems on our own, the road to change will appear to be blocked by a gaping chasm. By acting together on a communal scale, we can begin to find beautiful alternatives and cultivate collective power. The primary task, then, is not to change the minds of individuals, but to find ways to transform our shared lives that are sustaining and just. This shift also means that our primary shared work concerns healing our broken communities and ecosystems, rather than fretting over everything we must give up as individual consumers.[5]

The wisdom of the Psalms and the power of care are woven together here in the hopes that they may play a small part in addressing this time of ecological crisis. Our homes can become schools where we learn to live according to alternative rhythms and new dreams. Rooted in relationships of love, we can begin to incarnate cooperative communities that will yield grassroots power.[6]

Yet, if our families and homes are to become schools, this will require a complex pedagogy. In the midst of the creative and hopeful openings that we can find in relationships of love is all kinds of baggage.[7] The physical, moral, cultural, and personal architectures that mark our homes and our inherited understandings of family can often be obstacles to just and sustainable life. Of all people, parents are among those with the least energy to work for change as they try to keep their heads above water in the deluge of never-ending work and the second shift of caring for children.

The response here is neither to romanticize nor vilify homes, parents, or children. Rather, the hope is to nurture these spaces to multiply the different and life-giving forms they can take. Parenthood understood in this way is not limited to people caring for biological kin. Rather, it is a part of the great work of the future which Dona Haraway has called "making kin"—practices that expand our lines of care beyond biological relationships so that each child has layers of parents, the elderly are adopted by broad networks, and other webs of life might be regarded as part of our household.[8] Along these lines, parenthood does not serve as a castle fortified against the world, but it is a school, where we can learn to share the good gifts of creation with all of creation.[9]

The practice of praying the Psalms can help orient us in this work. In this book, I read the Psalms alongside traditions of Christian theology that seek in them the seeds of liberative wisdom and visions of a more just and beautiful world.[10] Yet, Scripture and Christian traditions are certainly not without their own problematic aspects. The meditations that follow seek to draw on elements of Christian theological and spiritual traditions that celebrate the goodness of creation, that seek transformation for justice, and that are grounded in a vision of covenant and the commons. These meditations also work to resist other tendencies[11] in these same traditions that are uneasy with bodily and social life, that counsel adaptation and acceptance to structures of oppression, and that are deeply individualistic and privatized.

As the author of these meditations, I do not pretend to be above this complex and critical pedagogy. This is not a book on parenting written by a renowned clinician or self-proclaimed guru. It was written from within the messy tangle of parenthood and seeks to learn from the ways of children, the practices of care, and traditions of wisdom. Freed from the fictions of the expert, where the author often pretends to view the world from above, these meditations are marked by the conflicts and folly that accompany my being a white, professional class, straight father. My hope is that these particularities and shortcomings are illuminating for readers in ways that are similar to that earliest of pedagogies—trial and error. This approach is one that I have learned in no small part from the Psalms, which consider matters of the utmost importance from below and in the midst of things—speaking in ways that are often stumbling, sometimes foolish, and frequently frustrated, as these prayerful poets struggle with themselves, their world, and even God to find paths of reorientation and refuge.

The lessons of this book do not provide blueprints nor are they performances that seek spectators. They are invitations for you to similarly weave together the Psalms and your own life. The central activity here is to expand the imagination concerning what is possible and to challenge us to think about what is truly precious and beautiful. The point is to redirect our hearts and habits away from pursuing false narratives of success and security, to instead follow that which is joyful and just.[12] This kind of learning is only gained by doing.

The meditations of this book modify the pedagogy of ancient practices of prayerful and personal reading.[13] Much of the power of Christian spiritual traditions comes through the ways that they weave together doing and knowing. In the Benedictine tradition, for example, one is constantly shifting between the central activities of study, labor, and praise.[14] Because of this, these activities inflect and deepen one another. Through this fusion a line of Scripture can follow a monk out into the field and shed a sacred light on the seemingly banal task of weeding the tomatoes. Here chores can be unveiled as labors of love that care for creation, creatures, and communities.

In a similar way the meditations of this book invite you to bring the Psalms into your life and to bring your life into the Psalms. In following the form of the braided essay, I attempt to model this interaction, reflecting on moments from my life as a parent alongside Scripture. The gambit is that on the one hand, this will bring the Scriptures into living color, while on the other it will reveal the sacred dimension of everyday actions, which are often superficially presented in the Technicolor of consumer culture.

Reading the meditations of this book is only part of the path offered. I ask that before you read each meditation that you read the psalm that is at the heart of the chapter. Keep the psalm next to you as you read, not because it is an object of study that will be dissected; rather, it is a companion that you will want to keep close. In the appendices I provide guidance on ways to prayerfully read Scripture. I also offer activities that will assist you in weaving the Psalms into your own life.

While these exercises can be carried out in solitude, they are also written to be used in community. It is my hope that this book can be read together by parent groups, Sunday school classes, members of an extended family, the proverbial village that supports a child, a cluster of houses, the elders of a church, a youth group, youth group leaders, the members of a community garden, seminary classes, and many of the other grassroots gatherings of people whose bonds of love hold the power needed to cultivate courage and hope.

These meditations on the Psalms encourage you into a practice of attending more closely to the wisdom that is hiding, like a bud, in the midst of our everyday lives. All it requires to blossom is the light of our attention, the nourishment of cultivated ground, and the flowing waters of shared love. These flowers of care will not only add beauty to our lives, but in time they will bear nourishing fruit. In an age of exhausted soils and exhausted peoples, in the face of planetary peril, one of our central tasks is to turn to those who are most precious and vulnerable in our lives, so that we can nurture them and learn from them.

Endnotes

1. Brueggemann and Bellinger, *Psalms*, 218.

2. This book was initially conceived as a companion to another book I have been working on for the past decade on the Psalms and dementia entitled *Singing the Psalms with My Father*. I had turned my focus to completing the former project just as the COVID-19 pandemic and the uprisings of 2020 began, which made the present work feel more urgent.

3. Attention to the everyday brings aspects of our shared lives that are often considered private or unimportant into the center of the craft of theology. I am indebted to Latinx theologies of *lo cotidiano*, yet my engagement with the everyday is from a decidedly different context. Isasi-Diaz privileges the epistemic position of Latina women in their tactical and strategic struggle against oppression and for justice. Isasi-Diaz, *Mujerista Theology*, 66–73. As she writes, "*lo cotindiano* is a powerful point of reference from where to begin to imagine a different world, a different societal structure, a different way of relation to the divine." Isasi-Diaz, "Mujerista Discourse," 49. See also Martell-Otero, "Satos and Saints," 10–11; Nanko-Fernandez, "*Lo Cotindiano*." By contrast, I engage with everyday spaces of professional class, largely white communities in the United States, seeking to interrogate places where they/we perilously collaborate with structures of extraction, exploitation, and oppression, and looking for promising openings that can lead to healing ways of life and cooperation with movements for justice. My work in this context is informed by both a critical strand of reflection on everyday life (like Anna Peterson, Keri Norgaard, Michel de Certeau, Michel Foucault, and Walter Benjamin) and Christian wisdom traditions that pursue exercises that subvert dominant norms and structures to open the path for a different way of life. See my account in Dickinson, *Exercises in New Creation*, 11–17, 61–63, 95–100, 124–130, 261–265.

4. Hawken, *Drawdown*.

5. I have explored this shift, especially in relation to the good news of Jesus Christ, that it is only by giving up our overfull, stressed, unjust lives in empire that we may save them, in *Green Good News*.

6. On homes and parenthood as schools of desire for public change see Peterson, *Everyday Ethics*. Similarly, Pope Francis extolls the power of environmental education, especially insofar as it engages habits and forms of life to cultivate solidarity, responsibility, and compassionate care, underlining the role that households and the care of children can play, and the centrality of aesthetic education. Francis, *Laudato si'*, sec. 209–15.

Endnotes

7. This work follows the long-standing eco-feminist insight that, as Sallie McFague proposed, we might seek to "become mothers and fathers to our world," so as to pursue justice through care and extending our sense of responsibility to all of creation. McFague, *Models of God*, 119, 120. Yet, as Bonnie Miller-McLemore qualifies, such a gesture will need to cultivate healing sentiments and practices in the face of all kinds of problematic models of parenting and family. Miller-McLemore, *Also A Mother*, 173. As Rosemary Radford Ruether envisions, it is only when families have addressed the structures of domination, oppression, and individualization within them that they can become sources of wider systemic change. See her *New Woman/New Earth*, 204–211; *Gaia and God*, 265–266. For a theological account of the transformation of patriarchal visions of family through an alternative vision of power, that moves across politics and beauty, to heal relational and communal life, see Brock, *Journeys by Heart*. For a postcolonial ecofeminist account that displaces Eurocentric formations of the household with the Korean *salim* movement, see Oh, "Salim, Women, and Oikos."

8. On making kin see Haraway, *Staying with the Trouble*, 2, 103, 209n18.

9. This shift in thinking about practices of parenting should be accompanied with a shift in our lived understanding of home. Siobhan Garrigan, for example, articulates a theological account of home that shifts focus from issues of belonging and identity, to being and longing, or intersubjectivity and desire, opening up a way of dwelling directed toward hospitality and solidarity. Garrigan, "Hermeneutics of Intersubjectivity."

10. With the formulation "liberative wisdom" I hope to name an intersectional space between several trajectories of figures and traditions. These different figures meet around the site of social reproduction—those practices, communities, and structures where we are cared for as biological beings and shaped as social beings (for more on this concept, see chapter 4). Around practices of care, education, and common life I stage a conversation between feminist traditions (Eco, Marxist, Transnational, Womanist, and others), liberation theologies, and Christian wisdom traditions. For an account of Christian wisdom traditions that counters abstract, privatized, and depoliticized readings by centering the practices of the care of the self, city, and creation, see Dickinson, *Exercises in New Creation*, esp. chapters 1 and 3.

11. I use the term "tendencies" to point toward the way theory and practice work together to shape dispositions to move and act in a certain direction—like tendons that join bone to muscle which are bendable. This is not of the order of logical necessity, but of power, capacity, and possibility. Dickinson, *Exercises in New Creation*, 95–96.

12. This work draws deeply from the wells of theological aesthetics and theopoetics. As Grace Jantzen proposes, at the heart of this approach is *how* we can discern the manifestation of the divine in the world and *how* we can learn to appreciate it. The emphasis is on beauty in the "daily round." *Place of Springs*, 50. Alejandro Garcia-Rivera says that the central question of theological aesthetics is: what moves the human heart? Or put otherwise, how can the human spirit receive divine beauty? *Community of the Beautiful*, 9–10. John Caputo proposes that a theopoetic approach engages with Scripture as "solicitations that call for a response . . . a style of existence, about a poetic possibility that we are invited to transform into existential actuality." *Weakness of God*, 117. Theological aesthetics and theopoetics weave together thought and action, divine glory and human praise, God's gifts of creation and the response

of liturgy and work, rather than separating them out into two worlds. This craft of theology is centered on the integrated, communal, creative, and embodied work of participating in shaping the heart—understood as the place of intellect, imagination, and desire. Roberto Goizueta's account of theological aesthetics, as rooted in a praxis of love and care, is especially helpful here. His theology of accompaniment is centered on the home, popular religion, and celebration—activities which are both an end in themselves and openings on the path to social transformation. *Caminemos Con Jesus*, chapter 5. See further Goizueta's critical account of suburban life in the United States (197–205). See also Keller, "Becoming of Theopoetics"; Thatamanil, "Constructive Theology as Theopoetics."

13. On the practices of reading and writing for contemporary transformation see Dickinson, *Exercises in New Creation*, esp. chapter 5.

14. For a broad spiritual account of Benedictine practice in everyday life see Chittister, *Wisdom Distilled*. On Benedictine practices of reading see Hollywood, "Benedictine Monasticism." For a survey of early Christian practices of reading the Psalms see Daley, "Finding the Right Key." The meditations of this book draw deeply upon various monastic traditions. Jean Leclercq notes that monastic modes of theology typically were articulated in the first person, expressed in a variety of literary forms, addressed to a specific audience pursuing a special way of life, and employed poetic imagery. Monastic theology does not simply instruct in knowledge but it seeks "knowledge through contact, the *affectus*." As Bernard of Clairvaux proposes, this is the wisdom "that touches the heart," the pouring fourth of divine love that prepares and inspires to action. Leclercq, *Love of Learning*, 4–5, 153, 214–215. Bernard of Clairvaux, *Sermones super Cantica Conticorum*, 23.14. Yet there are also many tensions with the approach I pursue in these pages and some of the central *tendencies* at work in these traditions. For example, the strand of theology championed by Athanasius that sees the Psalms as a way to teach us "how one must heal passion through speaking and acting," pursues a pedagogy and discipline where reason becomes "a master of its passions" that governs and demands compliance from "the body's members." Athanasius, *Epistula ad Marcellinum de interpretation* 13, 28/ *Letter to Marcellinus*, 112, 124. See also John Cassian, *Conferences*, 1.17–18. I share ecofeminist and womanist concerns that this pedagogy of mastery has deeply destructive and demonic consequences both for the people that pursue it, and for the peoples and places aligned with the body that this order also seeks to *master* (women, people of color, the poor, and creation itself). See, for example, Ruether, *Gaia and God*; Harris, *Ecowomanism*.

1—Finding Alternative Energy

Psalm 23

I TRY NOT TO cry in public, but it happens occasionally. Years of subtle messages about masculinity and professional propriety were nearly overcome in an instant as I watched my four-year-old son stand on the steps of the Kentucky State Capitol building during the youth-led Climate Strike in 2019. I felt a wave of emotion crash over me, as a problem that is planetary in scale was incarnated in the small, vulnerable, and beautiful face of my son. No longer did the destruction and suffering that accompanies climate change feel distant, but it was brought close and made urgent.

We had come to the protest largely at the initiative of my nephew Logan, who was fifteen at the time. Protesting at the center of power is one of the dominant scripts available for ordinary people to bring about change. Logan was excited to gather with others who cared about a matter that seems to be constantly at the front of his mind. It was an opportunity to finally *do* something.

This protest was not my first rodeo. I had been to these capitol steps many times, marching for climate and social justice. But in Kentucky, where King Coal still holds sway, I often felt a bit numb, if not cynical, at these demonstrations.

Something different happened when we handed my son and nephew the signs. When all the children and youth went forward and faced us, a different kind of power was harnessed. As my son looked at me, I saw with clarity the ways that I have been living in denial. I do not mean the kind of denial that rejects the reality of climate change. Instead, this is the denial that wants to be reasonable and so accepts the facts about climate change but does little to wrestle with the implications.[1] This is the denial that adds

1

changing lightbulbs to its overfull list of tasks, but refuses to challenge the habits, communities, and structures that are at the root of the problem. Seeing the faces of these teenagers and children—with furrowed brows brought on by the blinding light of the sun and emotion as they lifted their voices—served to disarm normal rationalizations. Because they were front and center, such thoughts of responsibility and complicity did not harden over into a self-centered shame. At stake was not my guilt or righteousness, but rather our shared future.

The hastily made signs that my son and the others held in their hands had the same slogans written on posterboard with marker I had seen at different marches, but the messages of protest felt animated with a new possibility, with an alternative energy. In front of us was the embodied reality that the future has not yet been written. If we had invited experts to show us charts and graphs, there would have been little cause for optimism. Instead, children and teenagers, who are often silenced, were given a microphone. Those who will be most affected by ecological catastrophe spoke up.

The most powerful moment of the protest was the least abstract. It was not just that children were on the steps. It was that Teddy was on the steps. My only, singular, cherished, frustrating, creative, hilarious, defiant son was a part of this assembly of and for the future. There is a power in the deep care and love that I have for him. It can be overwhelming *and* profoundly motivating.

Standing in that crowd and listening to those teenagers and children, I think I caught a glimpse of a path to a hopeful future. Their vulnerability called upon a different kind of life and movement. And yet, their fragility and the tragic scope of the problem also made me want to retreat or to at least numb out. I do not know how to walk down this path on my own, but we must find a way. There is no more time for denial or avoidance.

We cannot face a catastrophe woven into the natural, political, and economic systems of the entire earth on our own. Planetary problems demand collective responses. Though the individualism of our age might call us to examine our consumer choices as our only source of action, this is a dead end that will leave us exhausted and dispirited.

The term "carbon footprint" and the first calculator that invited individuals to evaluate their lifestyle choices was part of a marketing campaign in 2000 by British Petroleum. The implicit message here is clear: it is individual consumers who are both responsible for climate change and capable of solving the issue with their choices. The oil companies would have us believe that the source of the problem is not the multinational corporations that are pumping out millions of barrels of oil every day; it is you and your vice-ridden habits. Yet, as one study illustrated, the carbon intensive structures in the United States mean that even a person who is homeless—who sleeps in shelters and eats in soup kitchens—will still have an unsustainable footprint simply because of the economies and infrastructure in which they minimally participate.[2]

The supermarket and the suburb are not set up for sustainable living. While we are constantly presented with choices, they are often of the order of paper or plastic. Would you like to become entangled in deforestation or in products derived from petroleum that are filling up our waterways and accumulating in our bodies? While opting for canvas bags might seem like a solution, it does nothing to address the whole host of issues connected with what fills our bags. Focusing on your own choices while living in habitats designed for the opposite is like trying to dry yourself off with a towel while standing in a swimming pool.[3]

Even when we are able to make ostensibly sustainable choices, these choices often do very little to address underlying sources and causes. The gains that are made through more efficient use of resources or through behavioral changes often face what is called the rebound effect. For example, if large groups of people drive more fuel-efficient cars, but nothing is done to address the structures that produce and profit from petroleum, that will just mean that gas will become cheaper, and therefore, more attractive to other markets.[4]

This is not to say that we have no agency in the face of systems. We need to be able to change the structures that are the source of these problems. This will take both time and immense grassroots power. Furthermore, to build and sustain that kind of power the grass must have roots. We need communities that help us begin to incarnate the changes we want to see and that will cultivate long-term capacity to push for systemic change. Therefore, we need to look for practices and processes that enable us to live together in ways that are just and joyful. Transformed, beautiful, resilient, and just shared lives and communities, then, are both the means and ends of addressing climate change. They are both the purpose of our work, and they provide the broad-based power—the alternative energy—to get there. This is a vision of environmentalism and social change that does not ask us to tighten our belts and diet our way to a different future, but it is an invitation into different, delightful, and nourishing lives.

The path to this future, however, does not mean a clean break with our current contexts. Leveling the suburbs and skyscrapers to build new "green" communities would be a contradiction in terms. The road to a sustainable and just future goes through our current material and cultural realities so as to transform and repurpose them. This process, however, is incredibly complicated and more difficult than buying a new gadget. We will need a guide and a refuge on this journey.

The opening line of the psalm that is likely most familiar to us portrays God as a guide. The poet sings, "The LORD is my shepherd" (Ps 23:1a). More than offering a description, the psalm offers an invitation. It beckons us to join the poem in prayer, to make these words our words. We are invited not simply to read from an objective distance, but to get on our knees and to let these words pass through our hearts. We are encouraged to join a chorus that spans generations. In his fourth-century writing on prayer, John Cassian recounts the teaching of the Egyptian desert father Isaac, who says that praying the Psalms with our hearts is like a stag grazing on a nourishing pasture. This manner of reading the Psalms means that we take the disposition of the psalmist into ourselves, in part, by making the words and prayers of the Psalter our own. He counsels, "We first take in the power of what is said, rather than the knowledge of it."[5] Such prayer does not mean the suspension of the intellect, but it calls us into a space of intimate and vulnerable knowledge. There is a power that flows through these practical and spiritual exercises, if we have the eyes to see it.

This image of the guidance of a shepherd can help us to see the connections between what we might think of as private spiritual practice and broader efforts for social and political change. In the ancient Near East the shepherd denoted a sense of intimate care and it also carried strong connotations of political power. Kings were often spoken of as the shepherds of their people. Just bring to mind images you have seen of Egyptian pharaohs and notice that the rod they hold in their hand is the crooked staff of the shepherd. The king was a shepherd insofar as he claimed to offer care— feeding the flock and keeping the people safe. From the perspective of the sheep looking to the shepherd, one sees the promise of security and sustenance that fosters trust. But looking from the perspective of the shepherd to the sheep we can see how the shepherd step by step shapes the path and life of the sheep, exercising a kind of power that governs everyday life. With their eyes focused on the shepherd, and simply following well-worn paths, the sheep might not see how so many little acts—like pledges of allegiance, stories of success and security, regular assessments, and festival celebrations—shape their shared lives.[6]

The Hebrew prophets were quick to point out the differences between good and bad shepherds. Ezekiel excoriates the kings who called themselves shepherds, but only extracted proverbial meat and wool from the sheep. These false shepherds failed to feed the sheep, or to care for the weak, the sick, the injured, or the lost (Ezek 34:2–4). Sheep might follow bad shepherds if that is the only form of care and security they have ever known and if the whole flock is habituated into traveling down well-worn paths.

In the face of ecological catastrophe, how often have we followed the guidance of the bad shepherds that are leading us to ruin? In our work and even in our hopes and ambitions, how often do we follow their paths of supposed success and security? When we feel anxiety about our children's future how often do we focus on their education as a means to access the comfortable side of the gated communities of the coming world?

The Psalms are inviting us into a different way of life by calling upon us to truly pray that "the LORD is my shepherd." Could we pray this poetic wisdom into our lives and incarnate these words with our labors of love? What potencies might be hiding in this ancient prayerful poetry that could help us, personally and collectively, turn around and journey down another path?

From my own limited experiences, it seems that most parents actively avoid even thinking about climate change. When I am talking with other parents and it comes up that I am writing a book on parenthood and climate change, an awkwardness and uneasiness falls over their faces. I often hear things like, "Yeah, I should probably think about that more." The conversation quickly shifts to another topic. While I am accountable for generating a good deal of social awkwardness in any interaction, I cannot take sole responsibility for the anxious and uncomfortable avoidance I so often encounter around issues of climate.

I do not think this avoidance comes from a place of indifference. To the contrary, it is rooted in caring very deeply and feeling overwhelmed.[7]

The very same relationships and realizations that made the climate strike so powerful and urgent for me are also obstacles for many. Our love and care for our very real and very particular children brings fear into our hearts. In the face of our children the future is intimately close, and therefore so is the threat of the scarcity, loss, violence, alienation, fear, trauma, and suffering that climate change will bring.

To even begin to acknowledge the emerging realities of ecological disaster and to join in efforts to address them, we need practices and spaces that can offer refuge and reorientation.[8] The psalmist anticipates this need for comfort, pairing the image of the LORD as my shepherd with a promise, "I shall not want" (Ps 23:1b). That is to say, I shall not face a fundamental lack or essential need. This promise is not a matter of wish fulfillment that provides for all the desires of an unjust and misshapen heart. Rather, it is the promise that if we follow the ways of the good shepherd, we will find sustenance and security. As George Herbert rendered the opening verse,

> The God of love my shepherd is,
> And he that doth me feed;
> While he is mine, and I am his,
> What can I want or need?[9]

This opening line is a word of encouragement that cultivates the moral courage needed to turn around.

Psalm 23 continues by addressing our imaginations with images of simplicity and joy that help us envision what the way of life with God as our shepherd looks like. Keeping with the idyllic settings of sheep, the poet paints a picture that God "makes me lie down in green pastures." The poet continues coupling this sketch with the complementary and deepening image of "still waters" (Ps 23:2). The imagined ideal is simple and creational, a pasture and a stream that are a place for nourishment and rest. In the second stanza of the psalm, the poet adds another metaphor—the banquet. The Psalter calls to our mind's eye the image of God preparing "a table before me." God shows us hospitality, embracing us by anointing our head with oil, a culturally charged image indicating warm welcome.[10] The joy of this scene is underlined with the presence of a cup overflowing with wine (Ps 23:5). Here we are promised sufficiency. Not our cultural ideal of *self*-sufficiency, but rather an interdependent enoughness that springs out of right relationship between creature, creation, and Creator.[11] On this path we shall not want because we have learned the joys of rest, solidarity, and the nourishment of creation.

This path of simplicity and joy holds the promise of both my own well-being and the flourishing of others. As the psalmist sings, God as my shepherd "restores my soul." Robert Alter notes that the Hebrew word translated as soul, *nephesh*, would be more aptly rendered as "life breath" or "life."[12] The word is etymologically linked to the throat and has more an undertone of being a channel than a closed off, selfsame unity. The sense here, then, is God breathing life back into us. This personal restoration flows right through us and out into the world, as we act for the good and wholeness of others. The poet continues, declaring that God "leads me in right paths," in ways of justice (23:3).

We have a good deal to fear with climate change. This is especially true for younger generations and those who are yet to be born, who will face the brunt of this massive disruption of planetary systems. It is understandable that we would not want to spend our time focusing on the pain and suffering that will come, and this is even more so the case when it concerns those who we love most dearly. But to fail to face, much less act on, these problems only guarantees that our worst fears will be realized. Furthermore, insofar as we continue to act in ways that trust and serve the bad shepherds, we are only intensifying the destruction.

We must find a path that both faces these problems and points us to a just and joyful future. The psalm offers us this courage, leading us to pray, "even though I walk through the darkest valley, I fear no evil." The good shepherd is with us, God's rod and staff offer us comfort (Ps 23:4). By praying this psalm we may begin to speak where we have been silent, to pursue boldness where we have chased avoidance, and to transform our hopes and dreams to be centered on a world of green meadows, clean streams, and welcoming tables.

While my eyes were focused on my son holding his little sign of protest high above his head, I was also struck by the growing crowd of young people on the steps. Groups of children had walked in from a neighborhood school and dozens of teenagers had arrived on a couple of buses.

Following the typical script of such occasions, speakers eventually took turns addressing the crowd. Centering the voices of teenagers meant that there was a different affect and tenor to the talks. Woven in with policy issues were simple pleas for a livable future. There was also a more intuitive and felt sense of solidarity. While social divisions and even cliques are certainly characteristic of our teenage years, in the United States, there are few contexts where people are in closer proximity and more intimate relationship with others across lines of race, class, and sexual orientation than during our years in school.

I could not help but feel, however, that some of the energy of the event was dampened and dissipated by continuing to organize ourselves as speakers and spectators. Social movements have effectively used this format to direct grassroots power and to give coherence to a mass movement. But the breakdown of social structures over the course of the last half-century has meant that the grass has no roots. Yet we continue to use the methods of mass movements for small gatherings.[13]

Regardless of their efficacy or purpose, the energy of the talks and testimonies on the capitol steps was shorted out as the sky opened and rain fell almost out of nowhere. There were a few umbrellas in the crowd, but people soon dispersed. Our household gathered together and made our way to our car.

As I was strapping my son into his car seat, I could not help but think that I wanted there to be car seats everywhere. I felt danger and destruction looming in the future, a feeling I so often simply stuff under. I wanted as many five-point harnesses as I could find to secure him in for the rest of his years. And yet, this anxious impulse is no answer. A life strapped down in solitude is no life. Car seats provide limited protection in the midst of catastrophe.

What is needed is something more like the strange power that was conducted through the climate strike. We will find security in the future not by strapping ourselves and our loved ones in, but through turning outward and cultivating the common good. We need movement and collaboration, not fortified isolation. Perhaps most of all we will need the energy and potency of care, connection, and love.

As I got into the driver's seat and started the car, I wondered how I could take all of this home. How can I keep this realization of the great need of our times alive within me without burning out?[14] How can I care for my son in ways that will prepare him for the future? How can I continue the work that was called for by these children, to labor collectively to address such enormous problems?

The Psalms offer one such path. They can give us a practice that speaks to the full emotional range of a life of faithfulness. The Psalms can quicken our hearts when we are numb. They offer us words of assurance when we are despairing. They direct our hopes to simplicity and justice when we are led astray. They also speak with a concreteness that helps us see the sanctity of the everyday, which allows us to see the ways in which our everyday lives are tied up in cosmic dramas and animated by divine love. As Ada Maria Isasi–Diaz counsels, the Psalms can speak to the anguish we feel and sustain the hope that we need to stand in solidarity against broken and oppressive systems.[15]

Psalm 23 not only speaks of a good shepherd, but making its poetry our own prayer can serve as one. It reorients us to visions of sustenance and security that counter the offerings of the bad shepherds. Rather than seeking to hoard piles of wealth taken from others to assure our safety in the future, it leads us into the sufficiency of creation where we can live in simplicity and solidarity. If we follow this path, not only will everyone have enough, but we will have a joyful banquet.

The psalm ends by offering us this refuge. The poet sings,

> Surely goodness and mercy shall follow me
> all the days of my life,
> and I shall dwell in the house of the Lord
> my whole life long. (Ps 23:6)

This prayerful line directs our attention to the task of dwelling that animates every day. Our task is not simply to be occasional spectators at the centers of power. The good shepherd calls us onto the path of a transformed life. The psalm directs us to see the potential that is already flowing through so many other parts of our lives.

Perhaps the first task is to find ways to plant seeds of transformation in the richest soil of our lives—in places of love, care, and everyday life. This is a way of taking home the movement so that the grassroots can be rooted in ways that are sustaining, simple, just, and joyful.[16] The shepherd offers to lead us out of gated communities and into green pastures. While we might not yet have the courage to follow, the Psalms offer us exercises to find the strength to do so in the midst of our daily lives and our relationships of love and care.

2—Wondering in Creation

Psalm 100

I TOOK A COURSE in college on film that completely transformed how I look at movies. While I had been watching films my whole life, that class helped me see entirely new dimensions. The professor slowed things down and moved deliberately. Professor Fizdale would pause the film and ask questions about composition, like "What does it mean that this scene was shot in a way where she looks small?" or "Why is this flag in the foreground?" We would rewatch scenes several times, and he would ask us to think about why a scene of one character's failure was followed by a scene about another character's supposed success. The buttons on the remote served as imperatives that demanded our attention and action: "Stop!" "Pause!" "Rewind!"

Playing in the backyard or the park with my son is not unlike this course, as Teddy has taught me to see dimensions of the world that I largely ignore or have forgotten. He usually does not speak in abstractions about the beauty of the earth. He mostly speaks in imperatives. "Look at the leaves on that tree! They all have brown tips." "Lift up this rock! I want to see if there are any centipedes under it." "Stop. Look at those ants! I wonder what they are doing." His deliberate and patient lessons in the backyard, when I am disciplined enough to follow them, provide a practice embedded in a relationship of love and care that is profoundly reorienting.

Sometimes I am able to join him in this collaborative work. I might introduce him to one of our fellow creatures: "This one is called a walnut tree. That one is a paper tree." I might invite him to join me on the grass, in one of those brief moments of spring in Kentucky before the mosquitoes would punish such leisure, and direct him to close his eyes and tell me what he hears. We might gaze up at the clouds together and look for shapes.

These little lessons help me to look at the creation that surrounds me with joy and wonder.

While some adults are apt to look for nature in picturesque vistas that are far away, as Gary Paul Nabhan notes, children tend to look down at what is close and small.[17] In a similarly instructive manner, environmental justice movements speak of our environment as the places where we work, live, and play. Karen Baker-Fletcher combines these insights as she begins her theological reflections on creation remembering her childhood capacity to see the natural and social beauty that surrounded her in the neighborhood where she grew up. While classist and racist scripts might have portrayed the neighborhood as one that was downwardly mobile and subject to urban blight, she remembers a space of shared play and community with other children and other creatures. Grounded in this capacity to see beauty and possibility, she suggests that we begin with the places and homes where we were born and "where we live and work now." This rooted and grounded beginning does not mean the denial of local problems and systemic challenges, but rather it serves as a starting place where we can begin to learn and build communal capacity as we reach out to engage systemic and interrelated macro-ecological issues.[18]

This orientation of childish wonder and attention to the spaces where we work, live, and play helpfully counters many of the dominant narratives about the natural world that direct our attention to some pure or virginal space separate from human relationships. These are old scripts ranging from Henry David Thoreau's *Walden* to Annie Dillard's *Pilgrim at Tinker Creek*. Edited out of the frame of these compositions is that during Thoreau's self-sufficient solitude in the cabin, his mother helped him with food and laundry and that he regularly entertained guests. Similarly, Annie Dillard's poetic and mystical Tinker Creek took place in a suburb where she lived with her husband. There is a strange tendency in white environmental imaginaries to look for nature in places abstracted from our relationships of care and practical action. This leads us to imagine that issues of ecological catastrophe are primarily about something happening elsewhere, in the pure place out there that needs to be preserved, and that we relate to these matters as solitary individuals.[19]

Children, like justice movements, redirect our attention to that which is right under our noses, beneath our feet, and in our own backyard. Some of this is difficult to look at because it is broken or ostensibly boring. But children can help us see with curious and hopeful eyes. Our kids help us to see the wonder, beauty, resiliency, strength, and life buzzing and blooming in our midst. We need to be able to see this power flowing through creation and our common life if we are going to participate in the healing and transformation demanded by the ecological crisis.

Stop. Pause. Look again.

The poetry and prayer of the Psalms can also take us by the hands and teach us to see the joy of creation. Psalm 100 does just this, though it is a bit more focused on helping us hear. It begins singing, "Make a joyful noise to the LORD, all the earth" (Ps 100:1). This imperative is not just addressed to us, but to everyone and everything.[20] The psalm both calls for and directs us to the joyful noise that surrounds us. On several occasions my son has responded to the birdsong that fills the evening air wondering what they are singing about. My best and most frequent response is that they are singing praises to their Creator. Likewise, my son has paused before and observed that the wind blowing through the leaves in the trees sounds like clapping. The psalm echoes this insight and calls on us to see creation as a choir, and to contribute our part.

Like my son in the backyard, saying, "Help me reach this branch," Psalm 100 speaks to us mostly in imperatives. It calls on us to

> Worship the LORD with gladness;
> come into his presence with singing. (Ps 100:2)

We have to take time, in our relationships and in our bodies, to slow down, to be opened to the presence of God, and to sing praises. These are practices whereby we serve the LORD and are transformed.

Because the accounting schemes of our culture have devalued these kinds of action, the imperatives at the heart of this psalm might seem private or ephemeral. But there is something earthy and earthly involved in the imperative to worship. The Hebrew word translated here as "worship," *abad*, is the same used in the second creation story when the LORD gives humanity their vocation by placing Adam in the garden to "till [*abad*] and keep it" (Gen 2:15).[21] The term carries a deep sense of service and has a more holistic, everyday, and even political valence. We can hear this in Jesus' counsel that you cannot *serve* God and wealth (Matt 6:24).[22] James Mays notes that in the Exodus tradition, serving (*abad*) God is drawn in contrast to serving pharaoh. To serve God is to exit the pyramidal power structure of the empire and head into the wilderness and a different way of life.[23] In calling us into the joy of singing with creation, the psalm is directing us in ways that are practical, powerful, and countercultural. One of the ways that we till the garden, that we serve and worship God rather than money or the empire, is singing with gladness.

These imperatives mark a path that helps us to respond to the next charge of the psalm to "Know that the LORD is God" (Ps 100:3a). This imperative is a centerpiece of the poem. It is the fourth and therefore the middle of its seven imperatives. It serves as a hinge, and this lets us know that the other imperatives show us how to come to know God in this way. We make a joyful noise, we serve with gladness, we come into God's presence with song. We do not know a God that only exists in our minds. Nor do we come to know God through worship in a compartmentalized and privatized holy space. We know God when we have turned away from empire and serve God by following God's wilderness ways.

The verse continues and gives us a deeper sense of who God is and what it means to be in relationship with God. Characteristic of the Hebrew poetry of the Psalms, it works through a parallelism where related (often similar) lines are coupled together to add depth. This particular psalm works through triplets. The elaborations or siblings of the first imperative to know that the LORD is God underline the divine character as Creator and shepherd. These rich images bring our attention down into spaces that are rooted and grounded. The Psalter declares,

> It is he that made us, we are his;
> we are his people, and the sheep of his pasture. (Ps 100:3b)

This God is not abstract or aloof, and our knowledge of the divine is not something that we achieve after a long hike by ourselves and we see something picturesque far away. This is not the God who creates and then exits scene right. Rather, as the preponderance of possessive articles makes clear, "we are *his*; we are *his* people." Our relationship is thick and central. Or if we have ears to hear the particular phrases in this line, the relationship is covenantal.[24] We relate to God, returning to the beautiful pastoral image from the last meditation, as sheep to a shepherd. This is a relationship of care that concerns our sustenance, our security, and our entire way of life.

To follow and serve this God we should look to spaces of care, creation, and joy. This is not achieved through passive or disinterested looking, but these actions are done with others, all kinds of creatures, and all the earth. These are some of the actions that can help us see beyond the ways the empire has reduced our habitats to being natural resources, our lawns to be managed, or the commonwealth to real estate. Christ counseled in instructive imperatives that we might *look* to the lilies of the field and *consider* the birds of the air for these teachings (Matt 6:26–30). Perhaps we would also do well to listen to the teachings of children and attend more closely to the places where we work, live, and play. Perhaps part of our calling is to become more like them to enter into the kingdom—the cooperative commonwealth—of God (Matt 18:3).[25]

Stop. Pause. Read again.

On the occasions when I am able to follow my son's lead and really attend to the creation under my nose in the backyard, something magical happens. I am able to travel back in time. Echoing behind my son's laughter I can hear that of my own childhood friends. When I see him digging in the dirt it is as though I am looking at a palimpsest—my own infantile scrawlings in the soil are layered on top of his. These moments of wonder often help me connect with a past that typically feels lost—and this not only opens capacities for wonder and joy in my own heart but it seems to move outward as I can better discern the ways that all the earth makes a joyful noise.

This trick of time travel is a bit easier for me because we live in the house where I grew up. The yard has changed a good deal—the redbud tree I used to climb, the apple tree that was in the middle of the yard, and the thicket of honeysuckle that marked its entire south side are all gone—yet, an abundance of fecund connections remain.

These memories are often a conduit to joyful wonder, but they also often reveal the real losses that have occurred in the ensuing decades. When I was a kid, the four-and-a-half-acre lot behind ours was an open field with a thicket of trees in the middle of a small town. It was the site of many childhood adventures. Now this lot is crammed full of townhouses and a small gated community. The trees are gone, the topsoil is lost, and the impermeable surfaces of roofs and asphalt causes a yard down the street to flood regularly.

This change on this small piece of earth is representative of the transformation that has occurred throughout the county. During my childhood the town shifted from being a sleepy farming and college community, to becoming a Southern car manufacturing town. The construction of gas-guzzling cars also meant the construction of all kinds of houses and strip malls. Because both kinds of construction operations were focused on profit, this has not simply meant the loss of carbon-sinking fields and forests, but it has also meant creating homes for those who are wealthy and a lack of affordable housing for others. It has meant ecological, political, and economic problems that run off past the immediate attention of the affluent and that first affect other peoples and creatures downstream.[26]

To serve God, to live up to our vocation to till (*abad*), to serve the soil and God's good creation, we need to turn our attention to the places where we work, live, and play. At the heart of this work are the practices of singing and praise. By cultivating joy and wonder in our hearts and our relationships we can tap into the power that animates our world.

One day when I am attuned to the lesson my son is leading, and he asks me to lift a large stone so that he can look under it, I see, really see, the rich loamy soil that is revealed underneath. The roly-poly bugs and ants that skitter around seem to be dancing. This buzzing and beautiful life overflows beyond this moment and opens up memories. The last line of Psalm 100 comes to mind:

> For the LORD is good;
> his steadfast love endures forever,
> and his faithfulness to all generations. (Ps 100:5)

I try to hold on to this insight, to this joyful noise of the beauty of creation and the goodness and love of the Creator. But the last line strikes me. God is faithful to all generations, but how faithful have we been to God? What is being handed on to my son's generation? What will the effects of all the changes to this watershed, to say nothing of the global climate, be by the time he is my age? What of the generations yet to come?

Part of me wants to stuff these questions down and not to ruin the moment. But I remember that joy is not the same as happiness. Our joyful noises come not just from positive feelings, but also from the practices of faith, hope, and love in the face of fear, regret, and loss. I try to remember the lessons of my son and the imperatives of the psalm.

Stop. Pause. Look to the past. Think of the future.

3—Giving Voice to Muted Suffering

Psalm 13

SOME NIGHTMARES ARE SO vivid that they haunt you for the rest of the day. The waking nightmare that was the United States presidential election of 2016 still sticks with me. When early results made it look likely that Donald Trump could actually become president, I simply did not believe that was possible. My wife and I decided that watching this unfold was unnecessarily stressful. We went to bed expecting to wake up to better news.

We were both awakened a few hours later, when my teenage nephew, who lives with us, screamed and cried in anguish. Still under the haze of sleep I went downstairs to find the rest of our household sitting in a dark room slightly illuminated by the ghostly light of a television. What began as an election party had become something of a bedside vigil. My mom informed me that it was all but certain that Trump would win, though there might be a chance that Michigan and Wisconsin could go the other way.

I watched the television in disbelief. My heart and mind raced. I had already thought that a win by moderates would mean that we were in for the fight of our lives to address ecological catastrophe. In my head I started playing out scenarios. I was rehearsing all of the reports and warnings I had read about what would happen if we only engaged in half measures to address climate change. Now it was a virtual certainty not just that there would be a lack of action, but that instead already thin regulations protecting waters and workers, limiting emissions and drilling would be eviscerated. This shift in power would also mean the intensification of emissions and the organized assault on the structures of cooperation, care, and the common good that would make future resiliency possible.[27]

I can still vividly remember sitting on our couch, staring down at the black, white, and blood red patterns in the area rug. It was like I was staring into an abyss. Through my head rushed images of agricultural collapse—as droughts and floods destroyed already degraded fields and left behind wastelands. I saw hundreds of millions of people displaced by sea level rise, loss of access to water, famine, and deadly heat waves. I imagined the economic depression that would follow when creation, that we treat as both faucet (for resources) and drain (for waste), slowed to a trickle and became clogged. I envisioned the social conflicts, political destabilization, and war that would accompany all of this.

In the middle of these images was my year-and-a-half–old son Teddy. The macabre and devastating thought entered my mind that perhaps we had made a mistake by bringing a child into this world. Teddy had been an answer to our prayers. We had journeyed through the desert of infertility for four long years. He was most certainly a blessing. But looking at this future, thinking about the violent, cruel, and fearful world that he would face was too much. It was crushing.

I did not sleep for a couple of days. Gray hairs appeared in my beard for the first time. In my mind was a clear vision of what was coming, though my connection to the world became hazy. I had a hard time having conversations with people. I started what would become a habit for much of the Trump administration, constantly checking news sites, both hoping for a miracle but wondering if the looming cataclysm had started.

Over time, I began to get some sleep here and there. I slowly came back to the present. Trump's style of constantly stoking crisis and outrage, however, made it impossible to look away. It also helped to make it unavoidably clear that the problems that we face are not just in the future. Living and being shaped by a culture that makes economic inequality, the exploitation of peoples near and far, the desecration of lands, and the subjugation of women and people of color feel normal means that you develop all kinds of habits that help you avoid and numb out to what is painfully obvious. Trump's confrontational needling and unapologetic practice of saying the quiet parts out loud constantly disrupted the manners and norms of everyday white middle-class life. They made clear that we do not just face a threatening future, but a broken present, and an obscene and unjust past.

The dynamics of election night, however, would continue to play out in our household. In the face of unthinkably bad news, we would go to sleep, only to be woken up by the distress of a teenager. I would become overwhelmed by a world and emotions that refused to be easily managed. It was typically my nephew who would react in ways that were proportionate to the terrible news. I often lacked the capacity to join him or even to simply be present with him in these moments. I have been trained to only acknowledge and feel that which I can manage. The pain of watching a tragedy unfold in slow motion exceeded all of those coping skills and numbing agents. Yet, this pain also opened a door, and the only way out was through.

In the face of immense suffering and injustice it can be difficult to even begin to give voice to pain, because it might feel like a black hole. If we get too close to it, perhaps we will never be able to escape its pull. One response to this pain is simply to deny it, to create a shining space governed by the norms of comfort, cleanliness, and convenience.[28] This anesthetized domain offers the sheen of happiness, but more likely delivers numbness.

Dorothee Soelle called this cultural denial of suffering apathetic. Apathy, a word with Greek roots, means a lack of *pathos*, of passion and the possibility of misfortune and suffering. To avoid and deny suffering does not mean that we escape it. Rather, it means we fail to learn the cause of our suffering and that we become desensitized to the suffering of others. The apathetic person is someone who has become numb and has learned to accept things as they are, even if this acceptance largely functions as an uninspired indifference.[29]

The psalms of lament, however, give us words where we have been trained to be silent. Psalm 13 begins by inviting us to pray by questioning:

> How long, O Lord? Will you forget me forever?
> How long will you hide your face from me?
> How long must I bear pain in my soul,
> and have sorrow in my heart all day long? (Ps 13:1–2a)

This question takes us beyond silent suffering or even a wordless scream. It takes our pain and directs it to an addressee—God.

We are also given a refrain of frustration. Four times we ask, "How long?" Contrary to the norms of a world bent on management, that prescribes certainty and control, we are directed to speak into the space of uncertainty.[30] The question breaks through the resignation of the apathetic person. To simply begin speaking is to find an opening and movement where before we have been stuck. The medieval Jewish commentator Rashi drew out the wider consequences of these questions, as he interpreted each repetition of the question as addressing a different empire that had oppressed the Jewish people.[31] This question of "how long?" does not accept things as they are and pretend that this is the only way to address suffering. Rather, it breaks through this acceptance and looks toward an alternative.[32]

Knotted up with this frustration is the existence of hope that things will change. This hope is exemplified in Martin Luther King Jr.'s evocation of this lament in his speech that concluded the march from Selma to the steps of the Alabama State Capitol in 1965. He repeatedly responded to the question of "How long?" the structures of white supremacy would survive, with the response of "Not long."[33]

Not only does the lament of the psalm acknowledge suffering and yearn for a different future, but it also brings a struggle to the fore. We are directed to pray, "How long shall my enemy be exalted over me?" (Ps 13:2b). At issue is not something that arises from things as they are. The problem is not the impersonal laws of nature or the market, but there is an active conflict that is at the heart of the suffering.

The enemy named in the prayer carries with it a poetic possibility, and this vagueness serves as a pastoral opening.[34] While these enemies may be specific people, even such individuals are probably better understood as agents of particular forces, structures, institutions, and powers. In many early Christian interpretations of the Psalms these enemies were not simply seen as external to us, but they were identified as the ways that sinful structures colonize and come to possess our hearts, desires, and relationships. As Augustine comments upon this verse, this enemy could be the "habitual weakness of the flesh."[35] That is, the enemy named in our prayer and whom we struggle against could be the ways that images of success—subtlety premised on our competition with others and in service to institutions and systems that are plundering the earth and her peoples—guide our everyday energies.[36] These enemies can be at the same time powerful people, unjust structures, and parts of our selves.

How long will we approach climate change and systemic injustice as though they are simply problems to be managed, and which will not disrupt our apathetic order of comfort, cleanliness, and convenience? How long will our desire to appear buttoned up and reasonable, numb us to the sadness, anger, and outrage that would come from acknowledging the injustice and destruction? How long will we continue to engage in apathetic actions that pretend we can live sustainably simply by recycling the waste from systems that are tearing the ecological and social fabric to tatters?

The acceptance of the status quo, while it might make us appear at ease, allows the enemy to prevail. Our apathy in the face of both brash and subtle devastation allows the enemy to say "I have prevailed." The foes of life, justice, and joy "rejoice because I am shaken" (Ps 13:4). Psalm 13 challenges the resignation of defeat that our complacency announces.

The psalm does not direct us to take responsibility for our condition, to grab the wheel and steer ourselves back onto the right path. Rather, the poet directs us to look to that which is bigger than ourselves and our enemy, to call out to God. It functions under the audacious assumption that God actually cares. Such a cry does not numbly regard creation as fixed, cold, and uncaring. Rather it speaks in a deeply relational language. This pain is expressed in the image of God hiding God's face from us (Ps 13:1). The psalm petitions "*my* God" to consider, or it could be translated "to look" at me.[37] To gain God's regard would in turn, as the poetic coupling indicates, "Give light to my eyes" (Ps 13:3). Giving voice to pain in this prayer, far from drawing one into an abyss of isolation, allows us to call out to God to look upon us. This is a petition for a face-to-face relationship of care that would allow us to regain joyful and just life.

This petition breaks through apathy, as it is a protest against the current state of things. Challenging the status quo means losing many of our numbing agents. By moving through the pain, however, we can begin to see the sources of our suffering and can become sensitized to the suffering of others. These prayers of lament, then, are not a cathartic form of new age mindfulness that allow us to return to our work with greater patience and acceptance, but they are openings to compassion, solidarity, and new life. When we lament, as Emilie Townes writes, "we acknowledge and live the experience rather than try to hold it away from us out of some misguided notion of being objective or strong. We hurt; something is fractured, if not broken. A foul spirit lives in us and among us. We are living in structures of evil and wickedness that make us ill. We must name them as such . . . only then can we begin to heal."[38]

The often-named structure of the lament psalm lends itself to this movement. These prayers open in complaint, they articulate a petition for change, and end in an affirmation of trust and praise. As such, they give us not simply words to release the energy pent up from our mute suffering, but they give a structure and a practice that direct us toward transformation.

The shock, horror, and fear at the election of Trump kept me from sleeping for a while. I felt strained from the exhaustion. During the day I was numb, adrift, and distracted. It was like what was going on around me was muffled and hazy. At night, however, during the hours of black solitude and stillness, the numbness would lift, as I was left alone with my own piercing and haunting thoughts.

On the third night, I hesitated before I went to bed. I did not want to start the whole cycle over again by lying there with no hope of sleep. I thought that I would be better off distracting myself watching television or doing anything else.

Yet, after a couple of hours, I found myself stopping the spectacle. I wandered into my son's room. He lay there sleeping peacefully. His face was softly illuminated by a night-light that cast stars and moons on his ceiling.

All in a moment the pain, fear, sadness, and anger came rushing in. I lamented the losses that he would experience in his life. I wondered how long things would continue to get worse. How long would the legacies of oppression and injustice tighten their grip on the world? How long would God forget us? These emotions tossed and turned within me, as the tension was not simply between myself and an external enemy. The conflict reverberated in all of the ways that my life is tangled up with the brokenness—from the dreams I have for the future to the food that sustains me.

For the first time in days, I cried and I prayed.

The vulnerability that I saw in my son's sleeping face brought to mind the looming threat of injury. But that vulnerability also spoke to an openness, to the possibility of growth and the necessity of care.[39] Intertwined with the risk of injury was also the power of intimacy. To face such a reality meant both giving voice to lament *and* gaining the light in my eyes.

Swirling above Teddy's head were stars and moons projected by his night-light—a reminder of the vast scope of creation and the constancy of the Creator. Closed off to the ways of love and care, the cosmos can seem cold, distant, and empty. And yet, one does not overcome getting stuck in such thoughts by stuffing them under or avoiding them, but by giving voice to the pain, moving through it, and crying out for something else. Such exercises are not abstract or the work of isolated individuals. They are the prayers of people struggling in the messiness of life.

The lament psalms almost always end with a shift from petition to praise. The move often feels abrupt, and scholars have been at pains to explain the clunky transitions, frequently imagining the original worship context in which the psalms were prayed.[40] Psalm 13 is exemplary on this account as it concludes the brief prayer that began with so many frustrated questions, declaring,

> But I trusted in your steadfast love;
> my heart shall rejoice in your salvation.
> I will sing to the LORD,
> because he has dealt bountifully with me. (Ps 13:5–6)

Looking down on my son that night, I could feel this tension in my life. My love for him intensified the pangs and laments that held me down. But I also saw a path forward through the ways of love and care. To trust in steadfast love, to live faithfully, is not to calculate with certainty, but it is to proceed with hope in the midst of the pain. Part of this is possible because of the blessings that we have known. These blessings call on us to cry out and to sing. These cries and songs engage the parts of us and relationships that hold the power of transformation.

After having cried out in pain and feeling gratitude for the blessing of my son, I was able to sleep. This sleep was not refreshing and restorative but fitful. And yet, it was a start. Prayer did not allow me to escape the pain, but it did open the door to a different path.

4—Cultivating Peace and Power in the Everyday

Psalm 131

MUCH OF THE FIRST year of my son's life feels like a blur. I imagine that most of this is the aftereffect of complete and utter exhaustion. Not only was my mind, body, and spirit drained from a lack of sleep, but I think I was also dizzied and disoriented by the profound upheaval that becoming a parent created in the rest of my life. My relationship with my wife, my everyday rhythms, and my identity were all in transition. The changes were of such a fundamental nature that I think this time feels nebulous in retrospect because the everyday structures and patterns that had given my life shape and order up to that point were transforming. Things often simply did not fit together into coherent wholes or narrative sequences. The normal habits and rituals of my day were constantly interrupted by a cry for care.

Among a number of other issues, my son had an initially undiagnosed lip and tongue tie (a little extra connective tissue in his mouth that made it difficult for him to nurse). This provided an opening for me to briefly participate in his feeding time in a more bodily way. I would give him some of my wife's previously pumped breast milk from a syringe. This procedure required putting my pinkie in his mouth for him to suck on and placing a tiny tube next to it that would allow me to slowly give him the milk from the syringe.

I have several remarkably distinct memories of these times. I can still feel the soft fabric of the recliner I would often sit in, the strong suction of my son's nursing, and the ridge at the top of his mouth. I can see his eyes closed in concentration and his little button nose dancing as he ate. While such a moment is likely a shadow of the deeply embodied, immediate, and intuitive times he breastfed with my wife, there was a remarkable intimacy that came from providing sustenance in such a close way. I would always end these sessions by singing to him—songs that were so bone deep that my exhausted mind did not even have to reach for words, as I had sung them hundreds of times with my own father or around a campfire. Perhaps these times are clear because they were orienting moments of a new order of life, moments where our interdependence was incarnated and trust was being built.

Writing about this makes me feel as though I am intruding upon a scene that should belong to someone else. In many ways it does. I do not want to follow an old white guy script and try to appropriate experiences that are specific to women for myself. Embodied sexual difference and culturally powerful structures of gender importantly shape my relationship with my son in ways that are distinct from his relationship with his mother.

Perhaps this scene of care is vivid in my memories because it also performs a common cultural script about what care looks like. And so while I should be careful about claiming the role of mother for myself, I need not uncomfortably rush out of the room where a baby is nursing insofar as this reflex is rooted in thinking that labors of care, especially those that involve children and the home, are women's work.[41] This shroud of romanticized respect often covers over a general disregard that devalues and exploits such efforts. Attending to the wisdom of this scene could mean, instead, that I should look to other spaces of care—everyday tasks that gendered and economic pressures often push me to overlook, and that often happen in a blur or in the background.

Dwelling in this space of care may help those of us who are oriented by the goals and practices of a professional world to find another way to live. Learning from these spaces could not only help us to more fully respond to the needs of those we love, but it could also build up our capacity to hear and respond to the cries of the earth and her peoples. Perhaps these practices of care, that can be so disruptive to the smooth management of a way of life centered on productivity, can help us turn away from the structures that are at the root of so much suffering and destruction. Instead of trying to address the ecological crisis by working more efficiently within those same structures, we can begin to build communities that incarnate alternatives. By prayerfully examining these everyday practices we can begin to see tensions and fault lines in our lives that so often operate in a blurry background. And by learning from the creative and poetic possibilities of these relationships we can begin to catch sight of new, positive visions of shared life.

Psalm 131 is a brief song that attempts to orient us to the power, peace, and hope of attending to little things. The psalmist begins by making note of what she is focused on or oriented toward. The poet declares,

> O Lord, my heart is not lifted up,
> my eyes are not raised too high;
> I do not occupy myself with things
> too great and too marvelous for me. (Ps 131:1)

This string of negative statements marks a break in expectations. The heart, which in the Hebrew tradition is the seat of both intellect and passion, is *not* looking upward. The thoughts and desires of the poet are *not* striving toward something bigger and better. This sense of striving and directed activity is carried through in the final line of this first verse, as the Hebrew word translated here as "occupy" (*halak*) means "to walk." The path of the poet is *not* the ladder of success that leads up.

Ernesto Cardenal, in his poetic twentieth-century revolutionary rendering of the psalm, opens the prayer with a series of questions that give a little more flesh to what the psalmist might be negating. Cardenal writes,

> Lord
> do you think
> I'm ambitious?

Cardenal goes on to ask if God thinks he longs to be a millionaire or dreams of being "a member of cabinet." He continues by noting that he does not own the house he is living in, have a bank account, or an insurance policy.[42] John Chrysostom, addressing his congregants in fourth-century Antioch, underlines the ways in which the mighty and the marvelous are "rich, pretentious, and proud." The golden-mouthed late ancient preacher goes on to underline that this turning away from the haughty in humility is not simply a movement that one makes within, but that the psalmist is avoiding social relationships and gatherings with those who are wealthy and powerful.[43]

While these interpreters of the Psalms might be helpful in coming to understand what the prayer's attention is turning away from (ambitions for wealth and power), they often stay in this negative mode in imagining what they are turning toward. Cardenal focuses on what he does not have, Chrysostom focuses on humility and frets about not becoming prideful about a lack of pride. Chrysostom speaks of the image of weaning in the second verse (which we will return to briefly), in terms of Christ's affliction and crucifixion.[44]

It is telling of a tendency in many Christian spiritual traditions that even when there is clarity in the critique of power and wealth, there is sometimes a lack of vision as to what the alternative looks like. What does it mean not to look to great things? Is the only other way the path of humility, affliction, and the cross? While I think that some of this emphasis on negativity is grounded in a realism about the cruelty of the dominant order and the costs of stepping outside of it, I also fear that it betrays an uncomfortable desire to rush out of the room where children are nursing.

While the introduction of our son into our household disrupted just about every aspect of our lives, through countless new routines and relationships a new way of life took shape. Little everyday moments that I often overlooked as I rushed on to other things were brought into greater relief. Simple activities like getting dressed, eating, bodily functions, and nighttime rituals took center stage. My son's basic needs demanded energy and even strategic thinking. The maintenance of his cloth diapers alone virtually required a flow chart. Our daily schedule became organized around these rituals, and my relationship with my wife became centered on these tasks.

These everyday moments populate the rest of our lives but we are often too settled into them to notice. It strikes me that there are a number of similarities between the ritual of feeding my son and countless times where my family has said a blessing before a meal. On the occasions that we are all sitting down to a meal together, we typically say, "For health, and work, and daily food, and peace, and play, and friends, we thank God. Amen." That brief moment of joining hands and chanting together a prayer that we know by heart gives us all an opportunity to take the place of a dependent child in relation to God. The blessing is an opening to orient ourselves for the meal that we are about to eat and to recognize the ways that we are fully and entirely dependent, as creatures, upon creation. It is also a moment to appreciate the roles that we have played in the care and joy of others.

While such moments can be formative, this particular practice has become increasingly rare. There are many external forces that make sitting down together at the table difficult. There are time pressures from work and other commitments—when my wife might have to stay late at the hospital where she works or I might have to be present at an evening meeting—that pull us apart during this time. There are the complicated schedules of school, travel, and the demands of caretaking that mean that the mealtimes of our larger household very rarely match up. There is also the reality that even when several of us are present, that we are simply too exhausted to sit down together, and so we eat in shifts—while one person does chores and the other zones out. All of which is to say nothing about our ability to consistently engage in the joyful acts of cooking and eating foods that most fully nourish our bodies and care for the wider creation. This has meant that my son is probably more accustomed to seeing the television on during dinner than he is to hearing a blessing.

While I do lament the lack of consistency around the beautiful practice of saying a blessing and sharing a meal, I do not want to moralize about it. Saying a blessing is not a solution and its absence does not necessarily indicate the decay of the family. What these dynamics around the blessing highlight are not the individual failings of my family (or possibly yours), but the ways that economic and social structures form our shared lives—experienced through the demands of work, the kind of food that is available, and the expectations and desires of those around us.

Looking more closely at this everyday moment can help us reorient ourselves in what might otherwise be a blurry or forgotten domain. For example, even more telling than the absence of a blessing might be the ways that it feels hollow or meaningless. While cultural forces focused on novelty might make us think that this is because the prayer is said by rote, I would wager that the more likely possibility is that the words and the ritual are disconnected from the dominant features of our way of life. If the blessing feels like mumbling nonsense, that is probably because one is not at home in the world where these words dwell.

The everyday practice of a blessing might also be a place where we can begin to find connection. It could be an exercise that strengthens and affirms our bonds with each other, and our gratitude toward our Creator and other creatures.[45] Saying a prayer by rote before a meal together might be a concrete and specific way for us to turn our attention away from the mighty and the marvelous. Perhaps by turning our attention to this and so many other everyday exercises, we can begin to find avenues to live into another way of shared life in the midst of so many external pressures and tensions.

The central image of Psalm 131 is drawn from a thick instance of everyday care—a weaned child. The psalmist, no longer haughtily looking and striving toward that which is lofty, describes how her soul, her life, her very being has been smoothed and stilled. She sings, and invites us to pray,

> But I have calmed and quieted my soul,
> like a weaned child with its mother;
> my soul is like the weaned child that is with me. (Ps 131:2)

The child described here is one who has grown in trusting relationship with his or her mother. Though the child no longer nurses, the rhythms of that life, where the care of another has consistently provided comfort and sustenance, has fostered a trusting and patient ease with the world. It is not that the weaned child is now independent and self-reliant, with a good paying job and a mortgage. The image is not of a fully grown bird soaring in the air with a new mate, but of a fledgling that can fly but still hops after its parents, expectant of new lessons and food. The weaned child is not a being that has overcome and now forgets nursing and relationships of care, but a creature that has been shaped by and learned from the most intimate and direct care possible and is now coming to know the world through a life of shared love. The reorienting prayer of this psalm directs us to these everyday spaces of care.

And yet, many of the practices and expectations that shape our spiritual lives direct us to look elsewhere. In Christian spiritual traditions, the holy life is often characterized in terms that are specifically opposed to this scene of care. On this account, one comes closest to God in the solitude of the wilderness or with the door closed. Bonnie Miller-McLemore helpfully notes that this spiritual ideal is often connected with traditions that are uneasy, at best, with the busyness of family life, the messiness of bodily life, and the chaos of children. This leads many parents and caretakers to feel as though they are spiritually bereft and in need of carving out a time abstracted from their everyday lives that will allow them to become centered. By contrast, Miller-McLemore wants to redirect our attention, so that we look for the holy, sacred, and transformative openings in the midst of our chaotic practices of care.[46]

The psalm, likewise, guides us not to look to the mighty and the marvelous, but to instead look to the weaned child. While the poet speaks of their soul as a weaned child, as the paired couplet indicates, this state of spiritual well-being is understood by analogy to the specific weaned child that is with the psalmist.[47] The poet is not looking up for an exemplar, but right into the midst of her life shared with a child. The weaned child shows a path of trust and patience, earned through countless hours of comfort, sustenance, sharing, cooperation, and love.

In its closing line, Psalm 131 shifts from the intimate scene of a mother and a weaned child to all of Israel. This brief prayer concludes by singing,

> O Israel, hope in the LORD,
> from this time on and forevermore. (Ps 131:3)

The prayer initially followed a movement away from the expansive and the powerful, turning to the smaller and the intimate. In this closing movement, it turns back to the wider world, naming the collective of the people of the covenant. Rather than fixing our desires on the marvelous and mighty, it guides us to place our hopes in the ways of God.

This turn draws a parallel between the trust of the weaned child and the trust that the people should have in God. While such a move might tempt us to spiritualize the image of the child, and to lose sight of the concrete practices of care that can reorient our lives, the prayer seems to push us in the opposite direction. The psalmist returns to the collective, social, political, and economic horizon of Israel from the perspective of having found rest and peace in the practices of care. Rather than rushing out of the room in which a child is nursing, this prayer calls on us to emerge from these relationships transformed. They are not private and sentimental, and therefore divorced from what is practical and public. Rather, they can serve as constructive and generative instances of how we can become reoriented around hope and trust in God.

The positivity and power of this image of the weaned child is easily overlooked, in part, because these everyday activities of care are not included in our accounting schemes. The labor of taking care of children and the elderly, of keeping up a home, of maintaining friendships, communities, and neighborhoods, is unpaid and uncalculated.[48] Within our current neoliberal order what is counted is production. Feminists often refer to the sphere upon which processes of production and profit rely as the domain of "social reproduction." As Nancy Fraser explains, social reproduction is the care and labor that sustains us as natural beings and that shapes us as social beings. To put it in the barest of terms, you cannot have workers without housework. These communities of care include the home, educational institutions, neighborhoods, civic associations, and churches.[49]

Many of these spaces of social reproduction are buckling and crumbling under the freeloading weight of an unsustainable profit-driven machine that is trying to extract everything it can from its workers. Yet, there is also a power that is flowing through these communities of care. So long as our eyes are trained on the marvelous and the mighty, these domains of home, education, friendship, neighborhood, and church will seem invisible or at least nebulous. With a simple shift of attention, however, we can begin to understand that they hold the promise of transformation.

As Anna Peterson proposes, we could come to see our homes as schools of desire—as places that shape our hearts and hopes. Unlike the world of work, which is driven by the values of self-interest and privatized wealth, in many of our families and friendships there are stronger experiences of collaboration for the common good. These lessons could serve to build the capacity for rethinking our shared lives and broader systems.[50]

There are many overlapping movements that are currently pushing for a reorganization of the relationship between the corporate world that produces profit and the communal world of care. As Fraser underlines, this is what is at stake in "community movements for housing, healthcare, food security and an unconditional basic income; struggles for the rights of migrants, domestic workers and public employees . . . for a shorter work week, for generous paid maternity and parental leave."[51] Much of this is being led by people whose lives are centered on the work of care—nurses and teachers unions, migrant and domestic workers, and parents. At stake here is not merely a tug-of-war over what wages will be paid for an individual's work, a conflict that often accepts the underlying claims to property and power of the wealthy. This is instead a movement to reclaim our common life, our commonwealth, and the common creation for the care and flourishing of all. Informed by ways of life premised on nurturing, mutuality, equity, and trust, this critique of dominant forms of power and wealth is driven by a positive alternative vision.

Psalm 131 invites us to make the prayer of this mother our own. It guides us to turn away from the habits, goals, and gatherings of the wealthy and powerful. This little poem directs us to attend to that which is vulnerable, a child. We are to become like weaned children who have found, through relationships of care, the bonds of trust that allow us to relate to the world as a blessing.

Recently, our family has taken to singing a different blessing on the occasion that we sit down together at dinner. We sing a song that our son brought home from his Montessori preschool. The blessing repeats each of the following phrases: "God our Father; We thank you; For our many blessings; Amen." We have modified the prayer so that on the second singing we thank "God our Mother." Taken on its own, such a gesture could easily become an empty, self-congratulating edit. Yet, it also serves as an opening and a space of connection. By connecting the divine to the maternal we can begin to subvert the divisions that have rendered the domains of care insignificant. We can turn our attention to these spaces so that they are no longer presumed to be the work of women alone or a space of exploited and unpaid labor. We can also begin to learn from these practices and relationships of care to reimagine how our shared life and systems might look differently.

Left on its own, a blessing is little more than babbling. And yet, it can also be a place in our shared life where we hold hands and begin to work together to make a different life. This brief prayer could be like the babbling of a baby that is met with constant care and nourishment. Over time, the nebulous world around us might begin to come into focus as we find the peace and the power, the quiet and the calm, that comes to a weaned child.

5—Showing Right from Wrong

Psalm 15

MOST NIGHTS I WILL select several books from my son's shelves to read to him. Tonight he has beaten me to it, and is scanning the spines. His books are not a carefully curated collection. Almost all of them are gifts; some given thoughtfully and individually, others handed over to us by the armful.

We have not been entirely careless about what has found its way into this collection. No copy of *The Giving Tree* will ever rest on these shelves—that myth of perverse self-giving love and male narcissism that sees caring mother nature incarnated as a tree and reduces it to a stump. But there are plenty of his books that make me cringe. One, for instance, features a superhero named Michael Recycle who saves the day by convincing people to, you guessed it, recycle. There are certainly worse lessons to teach a child. Yet, given the steep uphill climb I face in my work in which mainstream environmentalism has basically told adults the same tale—that we can save the day by simply recycling the waste from an unjust and unsustainable system—I would be more than happy to grant this book its wish and put it in the recycling bin.

Tonight he selects *Our Two Gardens*.[52] I try not to flinch or show disapproval, mostly because such reactions only stoke his interest (a dynamic of prohibition and desire that goes back to that first of gardens). This book, told from the perspective of a young boy, begins by making a distinction between two gardens—the small one the is behind the boy's house that he shares with his family and a very big garden which is the whole earth, that he shares with everyone, and was planted by God. Following the pattern of the two creation stories in Genesis, the book initially paints pictures of the beautiful biodiversity of God's big garden, but then it shifts into an on-the-ground tale of fall and redemption. The main narrative is about a family that moves into a house with a nice garden that falls into disrepair—the apple tree and vegetable beds are depleted, there are bare patches in the grass, plants in the greenhouse and fish in the pond are dying. The family brings back the gardener that used to care for the yard, and she shows them the error of their ways—they were using too much weed killer, failed to pick up their trash, and so on. The gardener shows them both how these problems are taking place on a larger scale in the big garden and shares restorative methods for their backyard.

All in all, the book is not so bad. Still, I find it difficult to read to my son. Part of this is rooted in the book's concluding moral that offers hope for the "big garden" by imagining that perhaps the leaders of the world will get "embarrassed" and do something. This naivete is consistent throughout the book, as all of the problems of environmental destruction are portrayed as a result of individual actions that are largely based on ignorance rather than on unjust structures that necessitate exploitation and extraction.

Now if you are rolling your eyes at me for critiquing the "naivete" of a children's book, I will not stop you. This is a professional hazard. I cannot turn off my critical faculties. Maybe you could have a little compassion. Despite such absurdities, I want to persist in this critique for two reasons. First, the book is made painful by the fact that it was published in 1991, just a couple of years after the issue of "global warming" came to public awareness. This moment was a decisive turning point for the future of the planet. The leaders of the earth, in this case, showed no shame and instead followed systemic pressures to intensify all of the issues that were contributing to climate change. Rather than caring for the big garden, in the early 1990s those with power did everything they could to expand their small gardens, privatize everything, and deregulate the meager existing protections. To make matters worse, as Naomi Klein has demonstrated, the mainstream environmental movement signed off on it.[53] The failure in imagination portrayed in *Our Two Gardens* was one that was widespread and that had planetary consequences.

The second reason I find this difficult to read to my son is that the stories we tell are significant and formative.[54] We are surrounded by narratives that try to show us the path of a good life, that present an account of the difference between right and wrong. Sometimes these stories take place on scales that are cosmic and in ways that are spectacular (superhero stories are one of the few places where I can turn off my critical faculty, unless they

33

involve Michael Recycle). Most of these stories, however, are embedded in the everyday. This is something that marketers and advertisements have long understood. Ads often do not so much tell stories, as they use pregnant images that appeal to the narratives that have been hammered into our heads throughout our lives. To show an image of a house with a white picket fence, or its renovated equivalent of an open-concept kitchen with stainless steel appliances and a tasteful backsplash, does not require a story. We have already been told the story thousands of times—about how this is a domain of security, success, and self-actualization. Children's stories, likewise, move through the world of the ordinary; and through repetition, offer paths of meaning and value.

As I reluctantly read my son the book about the two gardens, I wonder how I can tell him a different story—a story that does not take for granted current unjust structures but which points toward another path. I at least have the good sense not to close the book and offer a lecture about the creation stories in Scripture and the failures of the environmental movement. But I do hesitate, as I do not fully know how to offer an alternative.

Psalm 15 paints a portrait of the path of the just who live in the presence of God. The poem offers us a vision of a good life in a few short verses, which we can prayerfully repeat. The psalmist begins at the threshold of the place where we can enter into the presence of God, asking: "O Lord, who may abide in your tent? Who may dwell on your holy hill?" (Ps 15:1). The responses offered trace a path back through everyday life. The poet tells us that those who can sojourn in God's tabernacle and enter into divine hospitality are:

> Those who walk blamelessly, and do what is right,
> and speak the truth from their heart. (Ps 15:2)

The verb tense in this verse indicates ongoing action. At stake is the way that an entire life fits together with integrity.[55] At the heart of this way of life is how we treat our neighbors. The poet adds to the initial three positive attributes, three negative ones. The person who can dwell with God is the one who does *not* slander, do evil to, or scorn one's neighbors (Ps 15:3).

The psalm presents an ideal image for us to pray upon and a negative one to avoid. The psalmist continues by noting that understanding this contrast is part of what marks the path of the just,

in whose eyes the wicked are despised,
but who honor those who fear the LORD. (Ps 15:4a)

The charged image presented by the poet assumes what Arthur Walker Jones calls an implied story that runs through the Psalms. The *wicked* are those who are rich, who have gained their wealth and power through deceit, violence, and the exploitation of the poor. The *just*, by contrast, are those who are honest, peaceful, and generous with the poor and vulnerable.[56] The wicked are cruel and clever. They are often the well-dressed servants of violent systems. In this way they are functionally atheists. As Patrick Miller says, they say "there is no God," like we might say "there is no food in the pantry."[57] They are not concerned with an abstract question about the existence of God—at stake is the presence of God. For the wicked, there are only two parties present in their daily lives, the strong and the weak. The just, by contrast, see beyond the struggle between the currently powerful and weak. For the just, relationships with others are triangulated by the presence of God.[58] This is illustrated in their practices of prayer, study, care, and justice. The backdrop of a beautiful and just creation animated by a loving Creator transforms the wealthy from being winners, into wicked exploiters that have made a mess of things. The repeated story in the Psalter is that these two characters are caught in a struggle. While it may appear that the wicked have the upper hand, the just must live according to the promises of God.

This story about the difference between right and wrong as they are incarnated in the figures of the just and the wicked stands in stark contrast with many of the stories of winners and losers that dominate our current context.[59] The narrative often called the American Dream has a very different vision of wealth and power.[60] According to this implied story, one moves up the ladder of success and the pyramid of wealth through talent and hard work. Those who fail to do so have only themselves to blame and are often the object of blame for social ills—as it is their ignorance and laziness that disrupts an otherwise just order. On this account the structures that organize our lives are largely taken to be natural and good, and the markers of wealth and success to be an indication of virtue and value.

This narrative of the American Dream is not so much a story told as it is one that is staged throughout our lives at pep rallies and award ceremonies, and is put on display in our clothes, cars, and job titles. It is ingrained into our hearts through all kinds of coercive measures like grades in school, assessment at work, in subtle social interactions, and the unsubtle demands of bills. According to the animating meritocratic story of the American Dream, those who are successful and powerful are those who are right and good.

The Psalms, however, tell a different story. Rather than winners and losers, they speak of the wicked and the just. This psalm's emphasis on doing what is right and telling the truth is *not* about following the rules and maintaining the status quo. There is an emphasis on speech here, on speaking the truth and not slandering, because there is an acknowledgment that the powerful often tell deceitful stories. Sometimes these lies are on the level of fraud in the marketplace, where the wicked might lie to tip the scales in their favor. These lies also extend to bigger stories that the powerful and wealthy tell themselves about how they have more than others because they are smarter and have earned it. The ideal of the just shifts attention from the accomplishment of the individual onto their relationships with others. The answer to the question of who can dwell in the presence of the LORD is largely about how people treat their neighbors.

Rather than understanding social, economic, and political structures as the playing field within which one wins or loses, Psalm 15 underlines the significance of power dynamics within them. The psalmist declares that the just are those

> who stand by their oath even to their hurt;
> who do not lend money at interest,
> and do not take a bribe against the innocent. (Ps 15:4b–5)

One is not deemed good by getting ahead, making a profit, or succeeding within things as they are. In fact, living a good life will mean missing out on these spoils—though it need not mean lacking a joyful and shared sufficiency.

This psalm provides a subtle little story that counters many of the dominant narratives of the American Dream that seek to shape our everyday lives. Now, obviously, this ancient poetry is not directly rebutting these contemporary cultural formations. Much of the power of the Psalter is the way that it speaks to these dynamics in different contexts. A midrash on Psalm 15—a rabbinic reading of the Scripture that tells the story behind the story and that reads between the lines of the biblical text—interprets the poem in terms of the oppressive force that plagued the lives of its readers.[61] In contrast to the just, the midrash speaks of "Rome, the wicked kingdom"—which gains wealth through extractive and unjust taxes, gains power through conquering other lands, and celebrates its own glory through statues. Speaking to peoples who are under siege from the false narratives of power and success of the empire, the midrash points to the prophetic promise that the ways of the wicked will not last, that their basilicas will be toppled.[62]

Basil of Caesarea, preaching to his fourth-century community in what is today known as Turkey, unpacked the significance of the poet's warning against charging interest (Ps 15:5a). He provides a number of brief vignettes that serve to reframe these practices of moneymaking to show how they are predatory. He notes that the one who is seeking a loan is in need and "he came seeking an ally but found an enemy." Along the lines of the repeated commandment of the Hebrew scriptures against such exploitation (Exod 22:25; Lev 25:36–27),[63] he warns, "though you have an obligation to remedy the poverty of someone like this, instead you increase the need, seeking harvest from the desert. It is as if a doctor were to go to the diseased, and instead of restoring them to health, were rather to rob them of the last remnant of strength."[64]

This simple act of producing wealth from debt, which either enslaves debtors through their labor or extracts their collateral, is not an isolated act. Basil points to its systemic roots, going so far as to say "borrowing is the origin of falsehood, the source of ingratitude, unkindness, perjury."[65] This practice of profiting performs the implied story of the wicked in which they pretend that they are the masters and possessors of the commonwealth of creation given by God. In the story of the wicked, we do not share the good gifts of the *Creator* in joy and compassion with others, but rather the wicked imagine that they are job *creators* and that they have produced and earned what they enclosed in their silos and bank accounts. This narrative of success and smarts supposedly entitles the wicked to power over others who have not done likewise.[66] This process of debt unleashes the power of money that "possesses [a] limitless ability to reproduce." Whereas creation is marked by limits to growth that allow for balance, the "monstrous creature" of debt does not.[67]

In stark contrast with the exploitative and extractive ways of the wicked, in his previous homily on the first part of Psalm 15, Basil underlines that the ways of the just are therapeutic and healing. More than simply resisting the wicked, the just are called to foster an alternative kind of community. He declares that "the Word challenges us to share and to love one another, in natural kinship." He holds up the ideal of the early Christian community told in Acts (Acts 2:42–47; 4:32–35). Instead of seeking to profit from the struggles of others, they gave what they had into "a shared supply of funds . . . so that it might be wisely and economically distributed according to the needs of each."[68] Basil draws upon an alternative implied story, which he repeatedly fleshes out in other sermons, of a loving common life grounded in the commonwealth of creation.[69]

It is this backdrop of the commons—of a beautiful creation equitably and joyfully shared among creatures with the love of the Creator flowing through it—that is so often lacking from our accounts of right and wrong. This often leads us to assume that the paths of piety marked out in the Psalms are about being good little boys and girls who follow the rules and obey the authorities. Psalm 15, however, tells us to speak up, even if it will earn us a demerit. To enter into the presence of God, and to live in the midst of the goodness of creation, we have to stop trying to win the games of profit and success. We must, instead, turn our attention toward caring for our neighbors and cultivating just communities.

Unsatisfied with our readings for the night, I try to adjust our story time syllabus. I reach for another book on the shelf—*A is for Activist*.[70] This book is an acrostic, a poetic form often used in the Psalter. Every line begins with another letter of the alphabet, and this is often said to give a sense of a comprehensive order. This book is an egalitarian ABCs, with each letter pointing to a facet of a justice-centered life, like

> G is for Grassroots.
> Sprouting from below.
> Sharing nutrients, and the waters' flow.
> Below the surface we're all connected.
> Stronger together—we Grow.

While I feel a bit better sharing this story with him, I know that lessons are not always positively received. Since Teddy was old enough to utter the word, he has always responded to the opening question of the book: "Are you an activist?" with a confident "No."

But as I read this book to my son, I am taken back to a time when I read it to a classroom of students as part of a college course I taught on "Theological Imagination and Social Change." During a session on the power of stories, I tried to evoke an old scene of instruction for them. I had the students circle around and sit cross-legged. I would show them the pictures of the book each time I read a line. I was a bit surprised with how moving I found this practice. It was the last class I was teaching at that college and many of the students were people who I had worked and collaborated with closely for four years. That moment made it clear just how embodied and intimate teaching is.

As I finish reading the book to my son, I think about how story time has only begun. I will show him the difference between right and wrong not just in what I read to him, but in the stories that I perform throughout my life. In her poem "On Memory," Emilie Townes recalls a time in her early childhood when she would walk from her elementary school and sit outside her mother's college biology classroom. Sitting there, she learned more than "technical biological tidbits" about "amoebas." Through her mother's precision, ease, and care she learned "to love learning." By watching her mother she was shown an exemplary path of care and attention that animates her own teaching. Townes points to this path through poetry, singing that in her teaching she wants to create

> an atmosphere that truly cherishes teaching and learning
> to care not only about ideas
> but the consequences of holding them
> of living them
> of losing them
> of gaining them.[71]

Yet, if I acknowledge that this longer story time is being staged every day, and displayed in the ways that we work and care for one another, I wonder what kind of a teacher I actually am. When I pray the Psalms that mark the differences between the wicked and the just, I do not find myself neatly on one side of that struggle.[72] The stories and ways of the wicked often guide my actions and sometimes take hold of my heart. The stories enacted in my life are not a carefully curated collection, but some of them are tales that have been thoughtlessly handed on to me and which I continue to incarnate.

As I look to my son, some of these neurotic concerns dissipate as I realize that he too has much to teach me. Perhaps it is in our efforts to care for one another, that we can learn the ways of the just. Nothing of Psalm 15 is about a life lived in independence or that involves standing above others. The poem concludes by promising that, "Those who do these things shall never be moved" (Ps 15:5b). This is because they are grounded and rooted into the presence of God in and through relationships of common life and commonwealth. This too is a story that has been handed on to us, and which we must learn to read and perform together.

6—Flipping the Script
on Success and Happiness

Psalm 37

MY SON LOVES MUSIC. As a toddler, he would instantly shift from being on the edge of open rebellion in a church pew during a sermon to becoming transfixed by the choir singing. Though our house is filled with worn toys and games, he has only been interested in one old collection—our CDs. He spends hours and hours in solitude exploring music and has even begun to perfect the art of making playlists.

While we have tried to nurture this ostensibly inborn passion, there are moments where I wonder if we have mis-stepped. By this I am not referring to his exposure to an abundance of bad to mediocre nineties music from our CDs, though this might be an apt illustration of the biblical adage that the sins of the father will be visited on the son. Rather, I wonder how often his creaturely gifts—which allow him to participate in the beauty of God's creation—get twisted and mixed up.

For instance, one day he and I were playing "band"—a game where we pretend to perform the music from one of his CDs. He was playing the drums on a variety of pillows surrounding him. I was pretending to play guitar. Mid-song, Teddy threw his pencil drumsticks in frustration and rolled on his back. He lamented, "I can't drum. I have to be the best drummer in the world!" For a while he was inconsolable. I tried to reason with him that we were just having fun, that five-year-olds are not supposed to be the best at anything, and that I as an adult will never approach being the best at something. I asked him, "What makes you think that you need to be the best?" To which he replied, "My [imaginary] monster friends said I

41

have to be the best drummer in the world. That I have to practice and work hard at it to become that." (This was during a very brief time when he talked about imaginary friends.) We went around and around like this.

There are moments that I can point to that helped to shape this line in his mind—that he had to be the best drummer in the world. The day before my brother Bart had been showing him videos of one of his heroes, a brilliant drummer who had just died. During that period Teddy had also gotten into watching children's baking shows, which would be innocent enough, were the children not bizarrely serious and the whole show not premised on discerning adults eliminating children until one emerged victorious. (As an aside, I will say that it has nothing to do with the fact that his father is a recovering workaholic. It is the television!)

What my son's outburst and these bizarre shows illuminate is not, unfortunately, an exceptional instance where a strange idea worked its way into his heart. These are full-blown social scripts that we are all constantly asked to perform. Though these scripts are not typically about being rock stars, there are all kinds of subtle lines and expectations that become written on our hearts about achievement and success. Sometimes they are explicitly named, like the tale about the American Dream mentioned in the last meditation. Often, they are more subtle. There are all kinds of monstrous little voices that whisper in our ears. It is these kinds of inherited structures and scripts that the biblical poets actually have in mind when they speak of the sins of fathers being visited on sons.

Teddy's first soccer practice was a mini-tutorial in these scripts. Each drill of the practice moved further away from cooperation and toward competition. While he understood perfectly well what to do when he was asked to pass the ball back and forth with a partner, he seemed to tighten up when they were put in a line and took turns shooting at the goal individually. He was downright confused when he was pitted against another child and instructed to take the ball away from the child and try to score it in the goal. He seemed legitimately befuddled as a child who he had never met before relentlessly kicked the ball in the goal over and over again. The other kid would kick the ball in the net, and then bring it out about a foot from the goal and kick it back in, even as Teddy disengaged. As the kids took a water break he came over to me, and I tried to explain, "This is just a different kind of play, buddy. It's okay to take the ball from the other kid. It's sort of the goal." As he was paired with a new partner, he did so. I thought I saw relief come over his face as he ran down the field with the ball. What he did not see was that behind him the little girl he had taken the ball from had gotten discouraged and ran off the field to sit with her parents. Something more than soccer was being practiced on the pitch that day.

While many of these scripts are often focused on our individual accomplishment, they have all kinds of social and structural consequences. These social scripts about success do not only place a great deal of pressure on the children who try to live them out, but there is also a slippage into scripts about supremacy. There is a *personal* trap in wanting to be *the* man—as in *the* man of the hour, or *the* big man on campus—in seeking fulfillment and acceptance through accomplishment and excellence. By definition, not everybody can be the best. Being above others is actually not a recipe for intimacy and love, but it is structurally premised on distance. Even more, there is a *social* underside to these personal scripts of success that are about being *the man*—as in the oppressive figure. This story of the upward mobility of the winners assumes a pyramidal structure with throngs of people on the bottom.

These scripts of success and supremacy are not simply played out on television or on the field, but they are subtly staged all of the time. Scripts of hierarchical domination are constantly staged in our lives, in terms of race, class, and gender. While we might not name it as such, children notice who does what kind of work in the house, or who is serving the food, stocking the shelves, and sweeping the floor elsewhere. We do not need to narrate these racist, gendered, and classist scripts for them, because they are constantly being performed.[73]

So many of these scripts of success and supremacy both lead us into looking for happiness in the wrong places and train our attention away from the injustice and destruction that they leave in their wake. These scripts make a world of winners and losers seem almost fair or natural, as imbalances are simply the result of talent and hard work. Performing these scripts means that instead of seeing systems that need to be cooperatively changed because they are consuming creation and God's creatures, we are led to try to gain happiness and love in the form of competing over the spoils.

Children, because they are still learning these scripts and have not fully accepted or memorized them, can help us see what we have taken for granted. In this way, they can reverse the scene of the previous meditation on story time, where as a parent I imagine that I can choose what stories I will teach to my son. In this case, Teddy teaches me the stories and scripts that I am thoughtlessly performing every day of my life.

Even more, because of their capacity for creativity, whimsy, and their sensitivity to beauty, children can help us flip the script. In his love of music, Teddy helps me slow down and attend to the beauty that surrounds me. He invites me into a space of collaborative play. In my love for him and in acts of daily care, I can begin to find different visions of happiness. Though I may be a little unpracticed in these scripts, they are not completely lost on me. I trust that they run even deeper than the ones of success and supremacy that have been whispered into my ear my whole life.

One way of looking at the lack of collective action related to issues of the ecological crisis is to see two scripts about happiness in conflict. The *primary* obstacle is not the skeptics who deny that climate change is really happening or caused by humans. This group has always been in the minority (albeit a powerful and well-resourced one).[74] Nor is it the majority of people who are convinced but largely unmoved.[75] It is that there are all kinds of scripts about success and supremacy that are actively moving us in the opposite direction. The *primary* problem is not that people lack information or even motivation, it is that they are *also* motivated and habituated to serve the very systems premised on exploitation and extraction that drive carbon emissions and the desecration of creation. This is perhaps illustrated nowhere more clearly than when we often address our anxiety for our children's future happiness not by organizing for justice or changing our lives, but by busily preparing them for an unsustainable and unjust world that looks like our own.[76]

To acknowledge this tension does not mean to take responsibility as an individual for systemic problems. Rather it is to begin to acknowledge the power that systems and social scripts have on our lives. Sarah Ahmed's account of "happiness scripts" is helpful here, as it underlines that we live in affective communities where the expectations of others, emotionally charged objects, and daily habits shape our lives.[77] We are not sovereign deciders who are able to freely choose and create the world around us. Rather, in addition to all kinds of structures, we inherit complicated images and instructions for what happiness is supposed to look like. These scripts are played out on the *social* stage of our lives.

In all kinds of little activities and in relationship to objects we are called to play a role. For example, with the consumption of meat—which is an enormous contributor to carbon emissions, deforestation, the suffering of creatures, and the exploitation of workers—there are all kinds of associations and social expectations.[78] We might associate a weekend gathering around a grill with familial intimacy and a rare break from work. This might mean that we buy a grill of our own and continue to cook meat in our pursuit of this promise, or that we have a duty to continue to participate in this practice with our parents on the weekends. We might gravitate to the grill not just because we like meat, but because it is supposed to hold the promise of the very things that are missing from our workaday lives—connection, rest, and delight. The task, then, is not to make a different set of choices as an individual, but to communally negotiate with these structures and scripts, and to work together to enact different ones.

Psalm 37 seeks to counter dominant scripts of happiness, success, and supremacy by addressing the ways that these scripts are entangled with everyday scenes where we care for those whom we love most deeply. Sometimes we might be seduced by the ways of the wicked out of our own self-concern or selfishness. Perhaps even more significantly, however, we pattern our lives after these performances because of our anxieties about the well-being of those we love, our sense of duty, and our fear of the social costs of stepping out of line. We do not want our children to miss out, fall behind, be excluded, ostracized, or exploited. Along these lines, I wonder how often I pass along little unconscious lessons about masculinity to my son because of fears like these. It is not as though we only play these roles after intentionally showing up for an audition and seeking a part. Rather we have been learning our lines since we were children. As adults they are inside of us at the level of muscle memory, like the lyrics to a song. We can probably feel them more in our gut than hear them with our ears. And so, the psalm offers us an alternative script, insight about our emotional response, and specific habits and spiritual practices to find a new way.

Psalm 37 is an acrostic that provides an alternative order. Its first three verses mark its central moves—as it names the problem of the supposed success of the wicked, warns us that they will reap what they sow, guides us on another path, and promises the coming of justice and the common good.

45

The poet begins by counseling,

> Do not fret because of the wicked;
> do not be envious of wrong doers. (Ps 37:1)

At the heart of the matter is the prosperity and luxury of the wicked (Ps 37:7, 16, 35). The dramatic production unfolding in our everyday lives seems to be set up so that they are the hero saving the day, the champion lifting the trophy, and the successful living in luxury. Their apparent success kindles within us an emotional response. The Hebrew word for "fret" (*charah*), which the Psalter counsels us against, means to burn with anger. It also carries with it a connotation of being provoked to imitation.[79] This is echoed in the couplet that warns us against envy. The poet is pointing toward an emotional scene of ambivalence where we are confronted with the excess of the wicked and are lured to follow a social script that would characterize their wealth and power as happiness and success.

The psalmist—returning to the implied story told in the last meditation—reminds us that the gains of the wicked are ill-gotten. Behind their fashion and finery is violence and exploitation. The poet dramatizes this by proclaiming:

> The wicked draw the sword and bend their bows
> to bring down the poor and needy,
> to kill those who walk uprightly. (Ps 37:14)

The wicked constantly turn to violence in explicit terms—paying the police to keep their order at home and the military to pursue their interests abroad. They also do so in implicit and structural ways, profiting off of the labor and debts of others. The ways of the wicked lead to broken bodies, struggling communities, and desecrated lands.

Yet, the dominant scripts that we are coerced to perform portray the wicked as strong, smart, and talented. The thing about scripts is that they tend not to be soliloquies. The stage needs players. To *not* say your lines and play your part is to step on the lines and undermine the role of others—whether you are a leading man or an extra. The wicked, then, violently protect not only their means to gaining wealth, but also the order that allows them to play the role of the happy and the successful. The psalmist acknowledges that there is a great deal of tension and trouble that awaits those who attempt to flip the script of success and supremacy, noting:

> The wicked plot against the righteous,

46

and gnash their teeth at them. (Ps 37:12)

The poet seeks to disrupt our envious imitation by warning that the ways of the wicked also lead to their own ruin. Their abundance is fleeting,

for they will soon fade like the grass,
and wither like the green herb. (Ps 37:2)

While much of this is due to the mortal character of all creatures, it is often hastened by the wicked because they fall victim to the violent order they serve (Ps 37:10, 13, 20, 35–36, 38). Following the aforementioned condemnation of how they draw their swords against the poor, the psalmist declares,

their sword shall enter their own heart,
and their bows shall be broken. (Ps 37:15)

The poet continues by declaring that the arms of the wicked will be broken (Ps 37:17). The image here is not of God intervening and enacting vengeance, but of the consequences of violating the created moral order.[80]

More than simply disrupting the supremacist script of the supposedly successful, the psalm addresses our hearts and habits. The poem names emotions that can serve as a hinge, opening the door onto one path or another. It points toward practices and small acts that can build our capacity to walk the perilous path to peace. The poet counsels us, "Trust in the LORD, and do good" (Ps 37:3a). This can serve as a counter to the anger and anxiety that accompanies living in the world of the wicked (Ps 37:8). We are told to refrain from such feelings by engaging practices of being "still before the LORD" and cultivating patience (Ps 37:7). Instead of looking to the bounty that the wicked have accumulated, the poet prayerfully directs us to look to those who live in peace (Ps 37:37). Learning to live in trust involves committing to the ways of God's justice through our actions (Ps 37:5). In contrast to the striving and straining that frets over the success of others, the poet charges us to center our hearts on the true source of joy: "Take delight in the LORD" (Ps 37:4).

The greatest tool of the wicked is not misinformation. Rather, they gain our collaboration through structures that funnel our labor and scripts that shape our hearts. And so, the psalmist does not simply charge us with resistance, but also with re-existence.[81] The poet acknowledges how the scripts of success and supremacy can affect us—stoking our envy, arousing our anger, and cultivating fear. Yet, we are also shown another path to peace and delight, one which we walk with each deep breath and committed act of justice. We flip the script by entering into a space of prayer and patience, which the world of the wicked can only understand as wasted time. Our attention is turned away from the successful and is directed to those who have learned to cultivate peace and to live through acts of love and delight.

The psalm seeks to direct us on this difficult path by pointing toward a promise that is in tension with the happiness scripts of the wicked, declaring, "you will live in the land, and enjoy security" (Ps 37:3b). Whereas the scripts of success and supremacy tempt us with being concerned with the inheritance of wealth that we can leave our children, the psalmist repeatedly promises that the inheritance of the land (*erets*, the earth) will go to those who wait, the meek, and the just (Ps 37:9b, 11, 22, 29). This is a vision lifted up by Christ in the Sermon on the Mount, quoting the Psalter that "the meek shall inherit the earth" (Matt 5:5/Ps 37:11). The term translated as "meek" (*anav*) refers to the "afflicted," "poor," or "oppressed." The promise names the problem, as Jose Miranda writes, that "the rich have seized the earth and are not permitting the rest of the population to live."[82] The poet fixes our eyes on an alternative hope, where an entire order will topple and the earth will be renewed by those who do not act with vengeance, but with generosity, peace, and delight.

Psalm 37 offers a vision of hope that can animate our *shared* lives. It promises us that the justice of our cause will be vindicated and will shine (Ps 37:6). The poet declares that the just and oppressed will not be put to shame, suffer during famine, be abandoned by God, or condemned when brought to trial (Ps 37:19, 33). In a line that has inspired the most skepticism by interpreters over the centuries, the psalmist declares,

> I have been young, and now am old,
> yet I have not seen the righteous forsaken
> or their children begging bread. (Ps 37:25)[83]

We do not have to look beyond our own communities to counter some of these claims empirically. Yet, the purpose of this poetic prayer is what such a script makes possible.[84] These images address the very anxieties and obligations that repeatedly draw us into following the happiness scripts of the wicked. It is not out of selfishness that we play along, but out of a sense of duty to others or fear for our children. The psalm directs us to alternative communal hopes. Martin Luther underlined that this is a shared hope, noting that the promise of inheriting the land (Ps 37:34) "may be understood as applying, not to each separate righteous [person] individually but to the group or community. Although some are destroyed for a time, their seed and their teaching will ultimately prevail."[85]

While we are constantly being called to envy and imitate the supremacy of the successful, the psalm disrupts the smooth functioning of a script that would have us think that the promise of happiness is tied up in wealth, luxury, and domineering power. The psalmist calls upon us to see:

> Better is a little that the righteous person has
> than the abundance of many wicked. (Ps 37:16)

The little of the just is a sufficiency that actually makes space. Seeking to simply have enough opens time in our lives for prayer and delight. Stopping with enough creates breathing room for other creatures. While one side of sufficiency and simplicity is about limits, the other side is about sharing. The simplicity of the just is better than the abundance of the wicked because the just "are generous and keep giving" (Ps 37:21b). As Luther wrote of this verse, what the just have is useful because it is "distributed to others" and is "not just heaped up." Thus, the just have enough and give their enough to others. While the wicked have a great deal, it is useless and "unchristian" because they keep it to themselves.[86] Our children will never be safe and will never have enough if we each have to have our own giant piles of goods hoarded behind high walls. What our children need is a healthy community and creation that can care for them, and which they may delight in caring for as well.

Ambrose of Milan, speaking to his fourth-century community, saw the path of simplicity and gentleness illuminated in this psalm as a medicine offered to ordinary people.[87] This therapeutic poetry counters the scripts of the unjust, that are often motivated by profit and plunder, with a justice that is more for others than oneself—a good for all which finds its reward in the good of others.[88] The psalmist tells us that the just "are ever giving liberally and lending" (Ps 37:26a). Ambrose clarifies that what is at stake here is not the lending of usury for interest, but "Christ's money" that lends in kindness.[89] This lending is grounded in a sense of the earth being a commons and the commonwealth given by God for all.[90] This vision of mutual care helps to guide habits of trust, generosity, peace, and delight so that we can find healing from the damage and destruction created by the wicked, including the ways that they have shaped our hearts. This script points us toward a path where we can seek security and joy.

When we follow these scripts of justice and share the commonwealth of creation, the psalmist tells us: our "children become a blessing" (Ps 37:26b). The Hebrew word translated as "children" (*zera*) also means "seed." This is captured in the King James Version:

> He is ever merciful, and lendeth;
> and his seed is blessed. (Ps 37:26)

There is an agrarian dimension of this poetic image. We find God's abundant blessing from creation—we find that our seed provides enough—when we share it among the community. We also find that our children will be a blessing, a prayer, a benediction when we give generously. Whereas the scripts of the wicked cause us to regard our children as a source of anxiety and envy, this script allows us to see them as the incarnation of the goodness of creation and the incantation of the blessing of the Creator.

My son's love of music is a blessing. The way that his heart is drawn toward the beauty of melody is a kind of prayer. Scripts of success and supremacy will guide him to channel these blessings for his own accomplishment—to find ways to make this beauty his property and to place himself above others as the best. This is a game, however, without real winners. It is a script that ends alone and anxious on stage—desperate to monetize its gifts. Or with instruments and dreams discarded and collecting dust in the closet. As a blessing, these gifts are meant to be shared. A passion for music could mean that one is not pushed to be the best but nurtured to be a conduit for the community. Such a script would not be centered on stars, but on the conductors who bring more and more people in to sing, to dance, and to share in delight.

This is the power that is also coursing through the Psalms. These prayerful poems, even when engaged in solitude, are addressed to social spaces and the scripts that we so often unconsciously perform. Like music, the performance of the Psalms is no mere intellectual exercise, but it is one that is also directed to our passions—giving voice to anxieties and fears, and inspiring trust and delight. The Psalms also sing of the promise of a beautiful life of simplicity and justice. They invite us into joining the chorus that will usher in this new creation.

Psalm 37 provides an alternative script, a different path for us to follow than the ways of the wicked. The poet offers us practices so that we can begin to redirect our anxieties for our children's future, cultivating communities of sufficiency, and seeking the common good. We can begin to flip this script by learning from our children—as they show us the happiness scripts that currently animate our lives and as they embody the blessings of God's good creation.

The psalmist sings to us the promise that,

> Our steps are made firm by the LORD
> when he delights in our way. (Ps 37:23)

As William Brown notes, the image here of the pathway to our healing and saving is one that is guided by God *and* characterized by our cooperation.[91] It is together, with the Creator, that we journey. We do not do so as individuals who stand above, possessing and controlling. Rather we do this as children of God. The poet continues,

> though we stumble, we shall not fall headlong,
> for the LORD holds us by the hand. (Ps 37:24)

To walk this path, we have to stop enviously reaching for the next rung on the ladder of success, and we must reach out to our fellow creatures and our Creator so that we may all inherit the earth and come to know the blessing that our children already are.

7—Crying Tears of Guilt and Hope

Psalm 130

ONE MORNING WHEN DRIVING my son to kindergarten, I fail to notice that the news is playing. We typically listen to music on the way to school. But on this fall morning, the news fills the car. The chronicle of tragedies piles up—a pandemic, racial oppression, and massive wildfires. I have become accustomed to such bad tidings, so I barely notice.

As we turn a corner, I am puzzled as to why the rising sun looks strange. It is as though there is a fog or a film over it. To my horror, I realize that the sun is cloaked by smoke from wildfires that are burning well over a thousand miles away. For a moment the pain breaks through. It is right in front of my face. The systemic brokenness is so widespread that it has blanketed the earth.

I reach to put on music. I hesitate as I wonder which of us I am trying to protect. Do I want to turn away because it is too difficult to face such unspeakable suffering? Do I want to drown out the bad news with music because my life participates in and contributes to all of these compounding plagues? How can I ever explain all of this to my son and give an account of what I have done, or not done, with my life to address it?

Changing the channel and attempting to create an alternative reality is, I think, one of the primary tactics of professional-class parents to live in denial about climate catastrophe and systemic injustice.[92] Sally Weintrobe calls this "climate disavowal."[93] It is a response that does not address a problem but stuffs it down. She proposes that because the root cause is never dealt with, disavowal is a process that intensifies as we must disavow more and more. This repetitive action has contradictory effects. As the reality of a problem is not addressed, the anxiety ratchets up and compounds. To overcompensate for the feeling of powerlessness that accompanies this, the person takes on an air of arrogance and almost omnipotence. This process leads to a disproportionality, as one feels both inordinately guilty *and* not responsible. For those of us who are white in the United States, we can see this dynamic at work as we disavow the structures of white supremacy and end up living in the mess of assuming that it is not our problem, feeling immense guilt, and occasionally pretending we are white saviors.

Climate disavowal is a process whereby we stuff down the scope and real sources of climate change. We cannot face how deeply the ecological crisis is intertwined with all of the systems and even the scripts that animate our lives. Our workplaces, our homes, and our retirement plans are all premised on calculations that are unjust and unsustainable. As a systemic problem, it is not as though we could simply choose to opt out of all of these and save the day. Rather we are entangled in them, and it would take the course of our lives and the collective action of many others to bring about transformation. This is overwhelming and terrifying. And so, we try to deny that it is even happening.

The truth of this injustice and destruction, however, confronts us every day in the news, in little interactions on the street, or in a brief moment when we can see the groaning of God's creation. To keep turning away, we have to disavow more and more. This stokes our anxiety and pushes us toward cycles of busyness and numbing out. My schedule is so full of tasks and meetings that sometimes all I have energy for at the end of the day is distraction on a screen.

To combat our feelings of powerlessness we might imagine that we are actually responsible and have some agency as individuals. Yet, this approach is a failure to face the systemic breadth and depth of the problem. We refuse to look at how climate change is rooted in our processes of production, accumulation, and exchange. We simply look at our own consumption, and fret over the labels on our food or the gas mileage our cars get. While such labors are certainly not without value, if they lack a deeper understanding and strategy of how these actions fit into efforts of collective change, then they are likely fictions that help us disavow the true source of the problem.

Throughout the day, I often find myself offering up little prayers for forgiveness from God. As I turn down the thermostat, as I hand my son a popsicle covered in plastic, or as I throw away some vegetables that have gone bad, I say in my heart "God have mercy on me." I do not think that this response is a sign of virtue or a practice that leads to healing. None of these petitions really get to the root of the issue. Instead, they seem to be prayers that are a symptom of disavowal rather than deep confession and contrition. They are the reflex of an inward-looking, guilt-ridden trap that keeps me from looking more deeply at the problem.

We need prayers that help us to name the problem with honesty. This will mean facing up to something we have been disavowing. We have been avoiding this reality for good reason. It is terrifying and confronting it will be painful. There are practices that can hold us and guide us, that will connect us with each other and with God. The practice of penance could help us to break the cycles of anxiety and guilt, so that we can begin turning our efforts to alternative hopes.

Psalm 130 has traditionally been listed among the penitential psalms. Cassiodorus, whose sixth-century commentary on the Psalms is the first place where the penitential psalms are named as such, says they provide a rule of prayer by which our hearts may be "pricked wholly by love" to find forgiveness and salvation. He goes on to say that praying these psalms is "life suitable medicine" from which we obtain "health-giving baths for our souls, from them we are restored to life when dead through sins."[94]

Psalm 130 begins with words that overcome the anxiety, avoidant shame, and apathetic numbness of disavowal. The poet declares, "Out of the depths I cry to you, O LORD" (Ps 130:1). The image of "depths" here calls to mind the chaotic forces of crashing waters and the pit—which in the Scriptures is the place of social and even bodily death.[95] The cry of the poet comes from a place without any sure footing, where solid ground has slipped out from under, and all that is below is unfathomable waters. The prayer cries out from a place of alienation and isolation, where the relationships that provide care and meaning have been severed, and God's presence seems to have slipped away.

This could be the cry of those who find their world shipwrecked, and they can no longer continue to tread water in their cycles of disavowal. They are coming to see the happiness scripts of success and supremacy as deteriorating driftwood. To acknowledge this reality, it can initially feel as though the foundation upon which we have built our lives is an abyss, that the relationships that sustain us have been lost.[96]

Though the prayer begins with desperation, it also points to a reorientation. The psalmist is turning from the threatening chaos to God. Psalm 130 continues:

> LORD, hear my voice!
> Let your ears be attentive
> to the voice of my supplications. (Ps 130:2)

The breakthrough of the initial cry has led to a different kind of speech. These are not words sleepily spoken in our Sunday best. There is a nakedness and honesty that marks this prayer. We are finally facing the sin that marks our lives.

Monastic theologians often have spoken of these initial movements of tearful penance as the affect of compunction. Michael Casey notes that the term *compunction* originally came from a medical context, "signifying a pricking, stinging sensation, or a piercing."[97] Compunction is like a lancing that releases a blockage or tension. The act of confessing one's sins and engaging in the work of repentance, repair, and transformation, is one that is marked by both pain and healing. The tears that well up in this process have a variety of sources. There are the tears of pain and fear that come from finally uncovering the source of our suffering. There is also the cry that issues from the puncture that comes from the efforts of the good physician. These are cries that mark the path of healing.

Breaking the cycle of disavowal does not lead to instant relief, because underlying these denials are real problems. And yet, it is also the case that we cannot begin healing until we are able to uncover the wounds and address their source. To do penance for our part in climate change will mean that we no longer nervously change the station and deny the suffering that we both feel and contribute to.[98] It will instead mean prayerfully confessing the ways that the material basis of our lives is tied up in systems of extraction and exploitation. This requires examining virtually everything—from the electronics through which we labor and distract ourselves, to the food that nourishes our bodies, to the houses and lawns on which we dwell. It is these systems that have oppressed peoples, desecrated lands, and caused the extinction of countless species.

There are initial tears and cries that come from this acknowledgment, as we see how profoundly we are entangled. We fail both in the ways we have not challenged these systems and in how we continue to serve them. We provide this service, too often, not out of reluctance but with zeal. We follow the scripts of the wicked hoping that we can gain security and some of the spoils.

We have to be careful, however, not to get lost in the inwardly oriented trap of self-blame as we make these examinations.[99] The healing that is available in these tears is the breakthrough of the blockage of disavowal through compunction. By acknowledging the scope and depth of the problem we can begin to untangle ourselves from the anxious busyness and exhaustion that comes from the contradictory knots of feeling not responsible, completely guilty, and capable of solving the problem through personal choices.

Psalm 130 gives voice to individual anguish, but it does so within a wider social context. As a psalm of assent, the sin spoken of in Psalm 130 is uttered communally.[100] This collective aspect of the confession is made clear by the final two verses, which are addressed to all of Israel (Ps 130:7–8). This prayer helps us to give voice to and acknowledge the depth and immensity of the guilt. The poet asks,

> If you, O LORD, should mark iniquities
> LORD, who could stand? (Ps 130:3)

Such a question is neither a disavowal nor is it the narcissistic obsession with one's own guilt. Rather, it is a confession of how deep and systemic the broken relationships between God, neighbor, and land are.

To give voice to the source of the problem and the part that we play in it can help us begin to see beyond it and a path forward. Psalm 130 does not end in guilt, but as Gregory the Great notes of the affect of compunction, the tears of remorse are matched by tears of hope, as confession can be met by grace.[101] The psalm marks this transition, noting that the relationship with God can be healed through God's mercy. The psalmist sings,

> But there is forgiveness with you,
> so that you may be revered. (Ps 130:4)

There is a change of perspective that occurs when one begins to look toward God and a broader social horizon. Rather than being struck by the awful depths that seem to open below us through the loss of the security that was promised by systems of sin, we can begin to become awestruck by and reverent of the expanse of God's love that stretches above us. These lines of the psalm shift perspective from an inwardly turned preoccupation with our faults to God's goodness.

This relationship of healing and forgiveness reminds us of the possibility of new life and change. The wider horizon opens us to the immensity, beauty, and resiliency of the Creator and creation. Whereas disavowal keeps us captive to anxious denial and focused on our own ability to solve things, simple confession turns us toward broken relationships and systems. Here the work is not simply to consume differently but to seek deep healing in our relationships and to transform our shared life.

The hope that comes from acknowledging the scope of systemic sin, the depth of our entanglement in it, and the avenues of divine healing demands patience. The poet declares,

> I hoped for the LORD, my being hoped,
> and for His word I waited.
> My being for the Master—
> more than the dawn-watchers watch for the dawn. (Ps 130:6–7)[102]

This attentive reorientation is made possible, in part, by the subtractive work of giving voice to the disavowed pain we have been feeling and the suffering we have been witnessing. On Luther's interpretation of this verse, this hope for newness is not unlike the work of a sculptor who takes pieces away to create a new shape.[103] Confessing our sin and the ways our lives are intertwined in sinful structures opens up space and the possibility that we could begin to chip away at the scripts that have shaped our hearts and the practices that shape our relationships.

Such change will take time and cooperation. The tears of joy and hope at the grace of God can provide us with the strength to live in this opening. Whereas our trust in the ways of the wicked might make this realization feel like an abyss, a reorientation to the goodness of God as the true source of our sustenance and joy can sustain us. As John Calvin says of this verse, the assurance we feel of having our "welfare attended by God" is "the mother of waiting or patience."[104]

By tuning out the world around us, keeping ourselves anxiously busy, or saying little prayers about isolated actions, we might save ourselves from a few tears. Penitent tears, however, can be healing. In these tears we might feel lost, adrift, and drowning. But in coming to face the systemic and social source of ecological collapse and widespread injustice, we can begin to take in a broader view. This view brings into focus broken relationships *and* the possibility that they might be healed in forgiveness and reparation. Attending to this relational space, we find both brokenness and new life. Living in this opening will mean leaning on God and practices that sculpt our hearts to be different. Along this path there are tears, but there is also hope that requires waiting and patience.

As I write this my son is only six years old. Climate change and ecological disaster are, at most, vague ideas for him. But I do sometimes imagine having to give an account of myself to him in the future. I do not think that my expression of guilt will focus on my choices. It seems absurd that I would sit down with a catalogue of my climate peccadilloes. "Son, I am sorry that on October 8, 2021, I turned down the thermostat. It was just so unseasonably hot and I needed some sleep." I imagine that the conversation will not so much be about me, as the world that I was tied up in. I think that the account we will have to give to future generations will be about how our lives got so focused on the efficient and productive working of processes that created profit and so much misery, how we became so busy and isolated, and how addressing big problems felt like a fever dream where we were groping for some kind of an answer but everything kept slipping through our fingers.

I am already having some of these conversations with my teenage nephew. Only the patterns of disavowal often take these conversations off course. They leave us at odds with one another, as my inaction is pitted against his desperation and deep feeling that he is responsible for solving this problem. We are often stuck in conversations about him trying to do his part by pressuring us to buy an electric car, and my responding that the earth is not alone in having limited resources. Lost in this exchange is that systemic problems rooted in issues of production, social reproduction, and accumulation will not be solved by individual consumer choices. What is needed is the virtuous circle of different kinds of lives and communities that build grassroots collective power that is capable of transforming structures that make more of these alternatives possible. We cannot get there on our own, especially if we are in denial about the reality that these structures need to change. But to face this frightening reality, we will need each other. We will need support, care, and love as we might feel we are free-falling into the depths as we lose the social scripts that call on us to trust wider unjust social systems.

Keeping this broader systemic and social horizon in sight is difficult, however, because the tendency to look at ourselves is produced by social practices that we engage in from church to work. Christian spiritual traditions are laden with the traps of individualistic habits of mind. As we go inward in prayer to lift up our thanksgivings and our confessions it can be easy to curve in on ourselves and to lose the world. The world of assessment has intensified this, as it constantly invites us into exercises that focus on our own performance. The genius of these little evaluation forms is that they exercise our muscles and tendencies toward self-obsession. Self-evaluation is a process where people can be made to feel responsible for realities over which they have little control.[105] The assessment form does not ask about broader workplace dysfunction, external time pressures, or if the tasks that the worker is asked to perform are reasonable, properly resourced, or achievable. The form creates a space where it is only you and your task.

This is why the BP marketing strategy that created the notion of the "carbon footprint," mentioned in chapter 1, was so wildly successful. Even people in the environmental movement jumped on it because we have all been schooled and shaped by these processes to look at our individual action. Professional-class people are *excited* to take these kinds of tests because these are the games we have been striving to succeed at our whole lives. But this framing of the problem makes us think that the solution is for us, as individuals, to ride our bike in a world made for cars. Because we have framed the issue in a way that misses the true source of the problem, these efforts of ostensibly taking responsibility are actually forms of disavowal.[106]

To transform our hearts and lives, which are shaped by these habits and exercises, we will need alternative practices to shift our attention and redirect our desire—practices like praying the Psalms. In turning to the Psalms to confess our sins we should not get stuck on our individual guilt. We should be drawn out to see the broken relationships that mark our lives. The puncturing of disavowal makes way for us to turn toward places of care and love to seek healing. Psalm 130 draws us into this social space as it calls upon all of the people of Israel to "hope in the LORD! For with the LORD there is steadfast love" (Ps 130:7). The psalm directs our hope to that space of covenantal love (*hesed*), of right and loving relationship between creature, creation, and Creator.

The poet concludes returning to the initial scenes of desperation and guilt. We are promised that the LORD will redeem us. The term "to redeem" (*padah*) points toward a process where one pays a debt on behalf of another to liberate them from bondage. The psalmist declares that it is the LORD "who will redeem Israel / from all its inequities" (Ps 130:8). That is, God will pay the debt and will relieve the bondage felt by the whole nation. The liberation here is one that is social and structural.

To acknowledge the scope of the problem, to stop trying to change the channel, to disrupt our tendencies to manage the problem in ways where we can assess and obsess on our own action is difficult. This confession implicates every part of our lives and can make us feel as though we are drowning. The task is not to disavow this situation, but to call out to God in contrition and hope. Doing so will open the path for us to be liberated from the structures of sin and the happiness scripts of success and supremacy that have ensnared us—and which are desecrating God's creation and creatures. While these practices of penance do not magically draw down carbon, they do allow us to begin to dress the wounds that mark our lives, relationships, and places. They open the path to hope that demands patience and that promises that God's redeeming and covenantal love can flow through our communities and lives.

8—Celebrating Holidays

Psalm 96

As a child I felt the expectation of Advent with my whole being. *Santa* was coming. Outside the upstairs bathroom, where my brothers and sister could see, we would hang a felt Advent calendar. Each day a dot would be added to show that we were one rotation of the earth closer to the promise of presents. Even before this calendar was hung, I would begin my holiday devotionals. While the family watched television in the evenings, I would carefully study a catalogue and put my wish list of toys together.

By the time we reached Christmas Eve, I was at the end of my patience. The day would drag on, and the nighttime vigil at church was almost too much. Why did we have to sing every verse of every Christmas hymn? In our house we had a rule that we could not go downstairs to see the presents that Santa had brought until 7 AM. I remember one year lying awake almost the entire night, staring down my digital clock. I was convinced that it was mocking me by occasionally moving backwards. In the darkness of the night my heart held steadfast to hope.

The hope of Christmas was partially about toys. I was craving the rush of dopamine I would get with the surprise and reward of unwrapping each gift. I remember the disappointment that would often set in soon afterwards. Coming down off the high, I would sometimes look around at the morning's spoils and think: "This is it? This is what I was so desperate for?" Other times, the disappointment was about realizing that I would not get another fix like that for an entire year.

There were other, less consumerist aspects of this hope that also captivated my heart. The new glut of toys meant new worlds of play. With my active imagination, toys were often a door into entirely other domains, which was partially about the excitement of adventure and the escape of fantasy. But even more, toys meant the joy of collaboration and creativity. I was the baby of the family and my siblings had pretty quickly moved on from childish games while I was still young. But on Christmas and with a new array of toys, they would often rejoin me in the play for a bit.

My childhood experience tied together deep feelings of wonder, familial connection, communal celebration, practices of devotion, and signs of faithfulness with the traps of consumerism. The wider culture told me that these connections came together like a beautiful red bow. As I got older, they felt more like "mind-forged manacles" that bound me to a certain way of life.[107] The challenge of Christmas was that family, faith, and the bounty of extraction and exploitation were so tightly entangled that it seemed as though to resist one you were resisting the others. These were not aspects that my parents chose or even highlighted. In fact, many of their efforts were focused on other parts of the holiday. The centrality of presents felt like it was imposed upon us by some faceless outside force.

Holidays could be otherwise. Festival time could give us an experience of a different rhythm to our days, of different bonds that strengthen our relationships, and different hopes that animate our efforts. To realize this revolutionary promise, we will need new rituals and practices that shape our shared lives. Our efforts to find this with our son have been both fruitful and fraught. The journey thus far has been marked by as many obstacles as openings to joy.

Psalm 96, a psalm often read at Christmas Eve and Christmas Day services, calls on us to engage our hearts and our lives in a different kind of celebration.[108] The poet opens with the charge:

> O sing to the LORD a new song;
> sing to the LORD, all the earth. (Ps 96:1)

The newness of the song is not about it being something freshly minted and straight out of the box. This new song is actually an old psalm, a poetic prayer handed down through the centuries.[109] The freshness of the song is the way that it frees us from the traps that have kept us from living into the full joy and flourishing of our life. As the couplet verse illustrates, this new song is, in many ways, the oldest of songs that creation has been singing since the beginning.

Implicit in the call for a new song is an acknowledgment of the power of song. Songs certainly contain ideas and values, but they are much more. They are charged with a beauty that connects with our hearts, pulls on our emotions, and directs our hopes. They call upon us to participate with our voices, and to learn through repetition and in harmony with others, so that the song can become bone deep and reflexive like muscle memory. Songs often dance with festival time as their cooperative power reinforces one another and shapes community. The Christmas carol that inspires joy and expectation as a child serves as a window in time when sung as an adult, so that our experience of Christmas each year is filled with echoes of years past.

Augustine of Hippo, guiding his north African community in his sermon on Psalm 96, mixes the call for a new song with metaphors of building. He makes this connection by drawing upon the heading that accompanied the psalm in his ancient Bible—"When the house was being built after captivity."[110] He notes that even with this heading, the psalm does not speak of hewing stone or erecting pillars. He suggests, instead, a figural connection, in which "to sing is to build."[111] Tying these actions together can help make concrete what might seem ephemeral or sentimental in singing and praise.

On this account singing is not reserved for the choir or limited to church, but it extends throughout our lives and works in concert with the entirety of creation. The Psalter calls upon us,

Sing to the Lord, bless his name;
tell of his salvation from day to day. (Ps 96:2)

This is a practice that gets into our hearts and that can animate our everyday action, turning it into a kind of testimony. Augustine again expands the action of singing, declaring that our "love is a voice that sings to God."

Our acts of love and the shared work of praise, then, serve as the brick and mortar that builds up the house of God. Augustine underlines the creational scope of the psalm and the active role creatures play. He writes, "It is the whole earth that sings this new song, for that is where the house is under construction. The entire earth is God's house."[112] The Psalter calls on us to sing a song of freshness and flourishing with all of creation so as to participate in the building up of creation.

Holidays and festival time are not simply private or superficial matters. These times when we both literally sing—and we engage in the proverbial singing of showing and sharing our love—are constructive. Each present is an act of sacrifice, where we translate our labor into a token of love that adds another stone to the foundation. Every holiday tradition serves as a bond with those who we hold most dear. This time of celebration is an act of praise where we show what we trust, value, and hope for. All of these acts serve to build up a temple—a place where we gather to sing to what we hold sacred and a space that holds us together.

While the psalm underlines the power of songs and celebration, it also warns that we can build these temples to idols. In contrast to the new song, then, are the old songs that worship the power and bounty of empire. Walker-Jones, reading the psalm within the broader context of the fourth book of the Psalms, proposes that Psalm 96 is a hymn sung from exile.[113] In captivity in Babylon, or in the captivity of so many empires that have followed, the old songs call upon the people to sing of the glory of the emperor and his imperial order. These old songs train our hearts into trusting that the empire and king are the source of security and blessing.

Psalm 96 contrasts the idols of empire with the Lord who "made the heavens" (Ps 96:6). The poet calls on us,

> Say among the nations, "The Lord is king!"
> The world is firmly established; it shall never be moved.
> He will judge the peoples with equity. (Ps 96:10)

Read from the vantage point of exile, this declaration of the kingship of the Creator is a counterpoint to the claims of the emperor. God is king, not any human.[114] God's creation is the basis of security and an order of generously administered justice.[115]

Augustine warns that if we do not sing the new song with all of creation, and "cling to fellowship with the whole earth" then we will not dwell in the house of the Lord, but in a "ruin."[116] In our observance of festival time, which songs do we sing? Do we sing the old songs to the idols of empire, that bear witness to the glory, security, and happiness offered by the great market? Do we dance in the ruins of exploitation and extraction and call them a temple? Do we join creation in its praise, or do we desecrate the good earth and focus on the plundered bounty?

If we have our doubts about which songs we sing during festival time, this psalm does not demand penance and sackcloth (a practice that certainly has its place, as explored in the previous chapter). The poet calls for the joy of a new song. But before we can begin to change our tune, we might first need to train our ears to hear the subtle ways in which these various songs have become entangled.

Before Teddy was born, I knew I did not want Santa to visit him on Christmas morning. I did not want to sing the old song with him and dress it up as a Christmas carol. Now before I go any further, I want to say that I have no doubts that others may have found many beautiful ways to adapt these traditions. Furthermore, I do not assume that by abstaining from one consumerist practice on one day of the year that I have obtained a righteous purity. Far from it. Rather, I think that our efforts to practice Christmas differently are illuminating in the ways it has been difficult, sometimes misguided, and often life-giving.

My initial desire to bar Santa from descending our chimney and lavishing my son with toys was an impulse that came at a gut level. The words that I found in trying to make sense of it were not entirely adequate. At first, I simply did not want the *footprint* that came with so much stuff. Connected with the newly unwrapped device, I could not help but see the gaping scars in the earth that come with pit mines, the broken bodies and communities of workers who were exploited, and ever-expanding greenhouse gas emissions. This felt like a perverse way to celebrate the birth of the Prince of Peace. The terms that often came to mind were about *consumption*, or sometimes other people would put the words into my mouth that I was against *secular* Christmas.

This framing of the issue led me to focus on limiting the number of presents and making an effort to center the properly *religious* elements of the season. But neither of these efforts seemed to be really getting to the heart of the matter. While the glut of things and trash that piled up on Christmas morning were not insignificant, taken within the scope of the whole year, it was an odd place to be putting my foot down. I would have found less resistance from family members, friends, and even complete strangers who ask my son what Santa is bringing him, if I had focused my energy on *any* other day of the year.

The issue is not just about the footprint of a few presents. Instead, the very things that make abstaining from Santa contentious and supercharged with emotion are the reasons for trying to sing a new song. Connecting the spoils of empire with expressions of love, stoking our lust for quickly discarded goods and calling it generosity, and reducing the song of festival time to a commercial jingle all powerfully shape our hearts. While these moments are not in and of themselves the sole sources of extraction and exploitation, they do play an important part in how this society reproduces itself. The present wrapped in family and faith has a profound multiplier effect throughout our lives. It also, in turn, shapes how we understand and what we expect from our homes, our spiritual traditions, and our festival time.

Addressing these relational dynamics is much more complicated. Limiting the number of gifts that we exchange is something that we can control. But finding ways to share our time and love differently takes cooperation, creativity, compassion, and patience.

While some people might hold onto Christmas traditions with nostalgia and happiness, others cling to them as numbing agents to deal with exhaustion, anxiety, and grief. As a recovering workaholic, I often collapse into holidays, approaching them simply as a time of rest that makes the rest of life possible. This approach means that I do not have energy to put much thought into what happens, and so I revert to familial and cultural defaults. For professional-class parents, staging the perfect childhood is often a way to deal with deep anxieties about the future.[117] Christmas can become a stage for a spectacle where we are all together in a picture-perfect morning in which we have provided for all of our children's wants and needs. For those whose experience of family is marked by trauma or loss, the ways that festival time connects us with the past can be haunting and overwhelming. This might make the escape into a commercial fantasy all the more alluring.

These dynamics mean that critiquing the dominant happiness scripts that are offered in the wider culture can be met with a layered and complicated hostility. This often leads to the dynamic where the person who raises the issue is made to feel that they have played the role of the killjoy.[118] Though climate change and injustice are systemic issues that affect all of us, because bringing them to light disrupts the shared performance of social scripts, the uncomfortable emotions that people feel become attached to the person who has spoken up. The global problem is transferred to being an opinion or property of a problematic person who is made to feel that they are ruining everyone else's good time. Recognizing these dynamics can help us to tread lightly, anticipate pushback that is personalized, and expect change to take a good deal of time.

Being against Santa has helped me to hear how the old song of empire worked its way into my heart, and some of the ways in which I am clandestinely called to sing its chorus. But this critical position is not much of a gift to pass on to my son. I do not want Teddy to associate Christmas with feelings of alienation and conflict. If we are to set limits here, it seems important to do so in order to make space for something affirmative and constructive. This is why we need to find ways to sing the new song, to share festival time in forms that harmonize with creation and that bring us together in joy.

The hinge of Psalm 96 offers us some directions about how we are to engage in this revitalized celebration. It paints a picture of a royal procession, but in so doing it topples the pretense of the spectacles of empire that attempt to claim glory for themselves. The poet sings

> Honor and majesty are before him;
> strength and beauty are in his sanctuary. (Ps 6:6)

This line personifies attributes like majesty and beauty as if they are courtiers.[119] They are portrayed as dynamic characters participating in a festival procession, rather than being properties that adhere to someone or something. This movement awakens our imagination to reconsider in what places we might find strength and glory and who exactly they might serve.

The psalmist then shifts to invite everyone into the procession. Specifically, the poet calls upon families to play a role. The psalmist guides us,

> Ascribe to the LORD, O families of the people,
> ascribe to the LORD glory and strength. (Ps 96:7)

This line parallels a similar imperative that begins Psalm 29, only that psalm calls upon "heavenly beings" to ascribe glory and strength to the LORD (Ps 29:1). Here the guidance is grounded in the activities and relationships of the household and earthly creatures. The poet continues,

> Ascribe to the LORD the glory due his name;
> bring an offering, and come into his courts. (Ps 96:8)

The King James Version renders the command as "give" rather than "ascribe," and thus in a rare reversal of roles, gives a more commonplace translation to the term (*yahab*). The repeated action that these verses call us into is one of offering up and giving over. Being a part of this procession means that we are participating in the acts of singing and giving sacrifice.

The psalm calls into our mind's eye a picture of families joining in a celebration of praising and giving presents. Yet, in our celebrations of Christmas, when we often sing this very psalm in worship, where are we locating glory and strength? In giving an article of clothing made in a sweatshop and with environmental impacts that include massive carbon emissions and water pollution, are we honoring our Creator, or are we locating beauty and majesty in the fruits that the empire has to offer?

To celebrate otherwise would mean to praise God the just Creator and to give presents to the LORD. Such a picture, however, begs the question: what do you give to the deity that has everything? Perhaps the best thing we could give to the Creator would be to care for her creation. The psalmist seems to provide a path here by declaring,

> Worship the LORD in holy splendor;
> tremble before him, all the earth. (Ps 96:9)

Walker-Jones suggests that a better translation of the term "tremble" would be "dance."[120]

The imperatives to worship and dance might seem to be trivial and ineffectual actions. They both mark activities that are difficult to monetize and quantify. To spend our time worshiping and dancing is to engage in activities that the empire sees as unproductive. These actions, however, follow the logic of the Sabbath, where we trust and honor God enough to stop, to rest, and to allow others to rest.[121] This cessation creates a space for us to attend and relate to our fellow creatures, creation, and the Creator in a different way. This shared time makes it easier to see the glory that exceeds our efforts to control and dominate, and to know the strength that comes through the interdependent care of the covenant.

Rather than genuflecting before the spirit of wealth or putting on display the glory and strength of the market, the poet calls upon the families of the people to ascribe, give, bring, come, worship, and dance before their Creator.

On Christmas morning, a couple of years ago, I woke up very early and could not go back to sleep. As this is a frequent occurrence, I did not fight my sleeplessness. I went into my office to read. A bit after dawn, I heard Teddy stirring in his room. As is his normal practice, he began his day by putting on some music. When the opening notes of John Coltrane's *Blue*

Train came through the walls, I thought to myself that this was a beautiful way to start Christmas. I gave him some time to conduct his morning ritual, and I finished taking my notes on my reading.

As I entered his room, he looked at me with what I call his morning smile. He has a particularly calm and peaceful look on his face at the beginning of the day. I think that it comes from time spent in stillness and solitude. It is as though he has been in his own little sanctuary, in a space of music and thought, where other parts of the world are sealed away and his imagination is able to flow and wash over everything.

Much of how our family has come to celebrate the Christmas season is about trying to make space for this very kind of spirit. While I have long been clear about my opposition to Santa, my wife Carly's abiding question has been: what shall we do instead? While I have spent time analyzing the underlying problems and sticky social dynamics, she has patiently experimented in alternatives. Many of her efforts have been to place greater emphasis on Advent. She has set up an Advent calendar in our kitchen that is a large wooden house, where each day has a door that opens to a compartment with a treat inside. On most evenings we have a brief time of shared prayer. Each morning Teddy gets a reminder of the sweetness of the season and each night we gather together to cultivate our expectant hope.

These small acts of disentangling festival time have helped me hold other aspects of the season more lightly. Whereas I formerly had to repress my inner Scrooge at the sight of a Christmas tree, I can now see that our artificial tree is covered with layers of memory in the form of homemade and passed-down ornaments. Even without the promised glut of toys, Teddy loves the decorations, setting up our creche, making cookies, and singing Christmas carols.

While there is still a small exchange of gifts between Teddy and my nephew Logan on Christmas Day, the centrality of stuff has been displaced by an opening of time. My wife and my sister Becky have worked to cultivate a joyful and playful character for the day. Our shared meal is now the centerpiece. The dearth of new gadgets and devices has helped to make a bit more space for listening, connecting, care, and joy.

Every year several of us will go for a walk in our neighborhood. Because we live in Kentucky, there are a wide range of possibilities as to the weather. Some years the ground is blanketed in snow, other years we do not even need a coat and the air is filled with birdsong. The alternative rhythms of the day often help me to hear the celebration that is always going on around me. As the poet of Psalm 96 sings,

> Let the heavens be glad, and let the earth rejoice;
> let the sea roar, and all that fills it;
> let the field exult, and everything that is in it. (Ps 96:11–12a)

If we have ears to hear and eyes to see, we will find that the new song is all around us. As Claudio Carvalhaes writes, "Our worship starts where we stand, in symbiosis with the earth, as humus, in love and reciprocity with the earth we inhabit."[122]

The power of festival time can easily dissipate with the day's end. Left in isolation, these practices might seem a bit precious. And yet, in the rhythms of these days we are offered a glimpse at another way of being. Whereas the workaday world sets our hopes on productivity and profit, and measures and shapes our relationships with expediency, during the holidays, we are able to dwell in a more sustained way in relationships of care animated by hopes of love and joy.[123]

Raquel Gutierrez Aguilar notes that people's movements can often feel like festivals. When they come from below, the upsurge in energy that drives people to take to the streets draws upon the same power. The break from everyday rhythms where people keep to themselves can often mean a breakthrough of a different kind of gathering. The inverse is also true, that festivals have a hint of revolution to them. She writes, "It happens that the time of rupture of everyday life, be it during a festival or a rebellion, is filled with what is collective, tumultuous, innovative, excessive, and dangerous. However, during the time of everyday life, everyone, each individual, each domestic unit, each community, union, neighborhood, or colony, is busy in their own way with their local productive and administrative affairs. In general this is based on repetitive and known behaviors that define this time as predicable and quiet."[124]

The new song that we can sing during the holidays should not be privatized and kept hidden within the nuclear family. Rather, in these times we can get a glimpse of rhythms that can change our lives, so that we can live in greater harmony with our neighbors and the land. Psalm 96 ends by training our hearts on such a hope. It promises that the Lord "is coming to judge the earth." Walker-Jones notes that the verb translated here as "to judge" does not draw on traditions of kingship, but rather it refers back to Israel's rulers before the kings. The judges were spirit-filled leaders that God would call up for a crisis situation. He translates the final line of the psalm that God will "govern the Earth community with justice, and the peoples with faithfulness" (Ps 96:13).[125] This is a hope that can more fully animate the rest of our lives when we have praised, ascribed, given, worshiped, and danced together in celebration.

9—Playing and Working for a Different World

Psalm 104

EARLY ON DURING THE COVID pandemic my wife, Carly, and Teddy made a blanket fort in his room. To get into the fort you had to crawl on your hands and knees. Inside there were piles of pillows and of various trinkets and treasures that Teddy had brought in. At times it would become so overfull that it was hard to find a place to sit. Given that the fort was located in his room, in his domain, Teddy established a number of rules. Central among them was that you could not get out your phone. I think his motivation for this was largely so that we could not take pictures, but it also doubled as a way of cutting out distractions. Throughout the pandemic we would occasionally erect a new blanket fort in his room or under the dinner table.

There is something magical about a blanket fort, as it creates a pocket of possibilities in the midst of the everyday. In there the imagination can run wild. The blankets are almost like blank canvases inviting one to paint on them—as it becomes a pirate's cove, then a castle, and then a house. This space is imbued with the power of transfiguration, as the enclosure, rather than confining, somehow opens up.

In the midst of the anxieties and exhaustion of a pandemic it was also a space of refuge and comfort. The fort created a world apart where the worries from the outside were softened, as we were nestled within the blankets. The pretense of walking tall was subverted, as you had to make yourself kid-sized to be a part of it. On our knees, we entered a space set apart—one which is holy, if only our spiritual aesthetic can be lightened enough to perceive it as such.[126]

In the blanket fort I find it a bit easier to enter into the world of play. I am not too proud to speak in a pirate voice around the house or in the backyard. I have done so often enough that Teddy has given us the names "White Beard" and "Fresh Beard." I will leave it to you to guess which of us is which. In a different space, however, with the rest of the world held at bay, it is easier to be silly.

In the space of play the pressures of productivity and efficiency are at least partially lifted. In this lighter space there is a greater sense of collective participation, whimsical engagement, and the centering of delight and beauty. While there are still certainly arguments and tensions—as my son is an only child and can be a bit tyrannical in our games and, as an older parent, I am often too tired to be an ideal playmate—there are openings for the imagination and heart to take flight. This flight could grant us a vision of a different kind of life, with collaborative relationships and joyful rhythms.

While the levity of play often transports us into the space of fantasy, more frequently children's play mimics the adult world. Even more often than playing the role of Fresh Beard, Teddy plays the role of a shopkeeper or baker. In this game, however, he does not simply rehearse the norms of the adult world, but they are put in a field of play where things are more malleable. At his bakery, he tends to give *me* money when I buy pretend pies. We are also able to exchange roles, pretend to do outlandish things, and laugh about it. In this mimicry of the adult world, roles are taken on in a symbolic way, are fiddled with, and discarded.[127] As Rubem Alves notes, in children's play roles and scripts are revisable, the future is open, and even in the case of imagined death, there is universal resurrection at the end. Adults, however, when they assume roles, tend to forget that they have been scripted by people and accept them as fate.[128]

There could be a flash of insight for adults that comes from the moment of invention in play. Entering into this sphere of playing roles helps us see the constructed character of everyday life that is so often controlled and constrained. This does not free us to act like we are kings at work, but it does assist us in seeing how contingent the rhythms of everyday life are and how they could be different. As Alves writes, "The limits of the social system define what is possible and what is not. In a society built upon the logic of war, peace is not possible. In an economy based on infinite growth, and therefore endless waste, ecological balance is not possible. These impossibilities, however, only describe for us the limits of the social order that creates them. Play, on the other hand, reveals that beyond the dissolution of reality, we find, not chaos, but rather new possibilities."[129]

Like the openings of festival time, simple practices of play can be transformative.[130] In our popular parlance, our workaday roles and scripts are referred to as "the real world." In moments of play with our children we can begin to tactilely engage with our hands, feel with our hearts, and see with our imaginations that another world is possible.[131]

Psalm 104 paints a picture that can transform how we look at and relate to our world. The poet begins by inflecting the greatness of God with some incarnational elements. God is spoken of as "clothed with honor and majesty, / wrapped in light as with a garment" (Ps 104:1b–2a). These images cause our imaginations to reach after heights that are not quite graspable. We begin to see the contours of something clothed, but this image does not settle. It slips as light dazzles, bends, and moves too fast to catch.

But with our eyes lifted up, the psalmist shifts our attention to see the Creator refracted through creation. The poet sings,

> You stretch out the heavens like a tent,
> you set the beams of your chambers on the waters. (Ps 104:2b–3a).

Here the earth is portrayed as God's home. The pocket universe created in our imaginations by this poem and given living breath through the practice of prayer is like imaginative play in a blanket fort. It provides an opening where we see that another world is not just possible but is already on the move.

The Psalter draws our attention to a world that is filled with God's activity and care. This Creator is no absentee landlord or departed watchmaker. Rather God rides on the clouds, sends word through the winds, and works through flame (Ps 104:3b–4).[132] Speaking in similarly elemental and dynamic terms, the poet also lifts up how God's care and nourishment flows over all of creation. The psalmist sings,

> You make springs gush forth in the valleys;
> they flow between the hills,
> giving drink to every wild animal. (Ps 104:10–11a)

God is not so much said to move above the waters one time in a primordial past, rather God moves through the waters that continue to well up and flow over.[133]

The poet tries to awaken our imagination and senses to a world that is filled with the wisdom of God. The Psalter declares,

> O LORD, how manifold are your works!
> In wisdom you have made them all;
> the earth is full of your creatures. (Ps 104:24)

Jerome, preaching in fourth-century Bethlehem, a landscape where incarnation is perhaps a bit more obvious,[134] notes how creation can help us perceive God. He declares in his homily on this psalm, "I see the trees sending forth leaves in their proper season, budding into blossom, bearing fruit, and I perceive the creator." These epiphanies in the everyday help us to see, in turn, the wisdom of creatures. As Jerome wonders, "When we perceive that the ant knows when winter is coming and stores away its food . . . the bee, and that it makes honey and wax: are not all these wonders worthy of admiration and are they not full of wisdom?"[135]

The psalmist imagines creation as the space where we work, live, and play—rather than as a standing reserve of resources or as a virginal wilderness. William Brown notes that the picture painted by the poet "is not so much a free range as a spacious home, and its inhabitants all share the earth as their common habitat."[136] The trees that God planted, waters, and cares for serve as homes for the birds. The poet asks us to make the prayer and song of praise our own that declares,

> In them the birds build their nests;
> the stork has its home in the fir trees.
> The high mountains are for the wild goats;
> the rocks are refuge for the coneys. (Ps 104:17–18)

This demands that we live into the reality that we share these spaces in common and in collaboration with other creatures.[137]

Yet, at the very end of the psalm, the poet briefly acknowledges that this is not necessarily how we typically relate to the world. The psalmist concludes this prayer of joy with a gesture toward the need for justice, saying,

> Let sinners be consumed from the earth,
> and let the wicked be no more. (Ps 104:35a)

Here we are reminded that the ways of the wicked often twist relationships of cooperation into exploitation, capture the waters of care as though they were a commodity, and desecrate the very house of God.[138] While another world is around us, our lives are entangled in ways of inhabiting and living that keep us from fully sharing in this truth, goodness, and beauty.

I often find it difficult to enter into the world of play with Teddy because my mind is otherwise occupied. Even when I am with him I often find myself thinking about the next thing on my to-do list. Sometimes I will watch the clock and worry about how I will fit all of my commitments into one day. Other times I will be contemplating about how to solve a work-related problem or ruminating on some dysfunction. I find that there is a whole host of obstacles to being present with my son, even when I am with him. Part of this is because playing with kids is not always fun. It can be boring and even tedious. But it also often feels like I am being pulled in another direction or I am out of step with the play. Sometimes it is as though there is a rhythm or drumbeat to my work life that is still booming in my head and chest even when I am away from my desk.

Many of the subtle messages I receive make me think that this is about me as an individual. I am told that I need to *manage* a work-life balance. But what this individualism and compartmentalization of work from life obscures is that work is much more than the hours we spend performing labor for a wage. Important though this is (and there is much to be done to seek justice and equity in this place), equally as significant are the ways that contemporary work is embedded within an ethic that governs our shared lives in specific ways.[139] This work mode is very different from the openings created by play, and it serves to guide our action and even to limit our imaginations, hopes, and dreams.

Contemporary work shapes our emotional lives and our expectations about shared practical action. Rather than reducing people to act as machines, contemporary professional-class work, for example, demands that we engage with our whole selves and with more and more of our time. The teacher, the nurse, the pastor, the executive director, the project manager, the case worker, and so on are all called upon to give of themselves, to care, to think creatively, and to thrive as part of a team.[140] Yet, our emotional connections with work must be *managed*. The ethos of the workplace demands that thick emotions associated with dependence and intimacy need

9—Playing and Working for a Different World

to be held at bay. Rather, we are called to engage with passion and creativity in a distanced and controlled way.[141] Even more important, our experience of collaborating with others is guided by the values of efficiency and productivity that are directed toward the bottom line of the organization and our own career advancement.

This work culture shapes the emotional range and cooperative goals of what we might think of as our personal lives. We can see this most obviously in therapeutic inventories or exercises that invite us to control our emotions by distancing ourselves from them. We are trained not to identify with our sadness but to name it and observe it. These techniques call upon us to play the role of a manager who clarifies values and goals, assesses choices, and makes a preferred course of action.[142] We are also guided to view our kids as emerging forms of human capital, whose earning potential we need to cultivate through education—getting them the access to the right schools, shaping their capacities, and managing their time through private lessons, sports, and other activities.[143] Here we work together so that they can win at life by securing a high-paying job with fulfilling work in a competitive marketplace.

Being so deeply engaged in these practices with so much of our lives serves to shape our hearts and the norms and rituals that structure our communities. The day-in, day-out work in this *shared* space and the constant discipline of carrot and stick narrow the range of emotions that we find acceptable in ourselves and others. A focus on productivity, efficiency, and short-term measurable outcomes also trains us to rush toward clear and achievable tasks, while more complicated, long-term, and nebulous actions are cast aside. A focus on the bottom line and our own assessment also serves to narrow our imaginations and dreams, limiting what we find to be practical, possible, and perhaps even desirable.

A complicated, long-term, systemic, and transformational problem like climate change completely short-circuits the communal capacities of this work culture. The emotions that climate change evokes—with feelings of guilt, despair, and anxiety—threaten to exceed the agreeable and managed disposition that is expected of us. The governing norms that constantly demand we look back to our own action and question what we can do in an efficient and achievable way are shattered in the face of *planetary* problems. This is not an issue that can be addressed within the time that we have allotted for our meeting (or possibly the time we have left in our lives). To ponder it would be to undermine our current plans and question our governing values. To face this challenge would demand a kind of intense vulnerability, uncertainty, and patience that is simply unthinkable.[144] It falls so far out of the bounds of what we are trained to *manage*, that we might avoid it entirely or attempt to cut it down to a size that a committee can address before the hour is up. Nobody panic, we can manage this and feel calm, collected, and in control. We have agreed to use biodegradable straws. What is the next item on the agenda?

From the vantage point of this work ethic, playing with our children might feel like an idle or indulgent waste of time. Yet, this is in no small part because play challenges its norms, emotional range, and goals. Precisely because they challenge these limiting norms and goals, times of play might be helpful for cultivating part of what we need to face our shared problems.[145]

The unhurried pace of children, as Miller-McLemore notes, undercuts norms and assumptions that reduce generativity to a certain kind of productivity.[146] The rush to maximize the amount that each moment and action can produce is tripped up by the child who will not stop chasing a butterfly to get in his car seat, or who has been staring out the window instead of putting on her socks. While the work mode will only experience this as frustration, any time that we can spend walking alongside our children may be instructive. Letting the seconds slip by can help cultivate patience, open space for creativity, and engender a capacity to attend to what is typically ignored, looked over, and stepped on.

In the space of play and in time with children we can find a different quality of relationships, as our shared action is focused on reciprocity, intimacy, and aesthetic pleasure over profit, time management, and efficiency.[147] These bonds help shape a space in which we can more fully dwell with and move through emotions that might otherwise feel unmanageable or shameful. While it is outside the bounds of the game of tag to openly weep, time to laugh and wonder can create a kind of breathing room. These times and spaces can help us center relationships of care. Though these norms and relationships are completely left out of the accounting and assessment of the work ethic, they are the life blood of community and collective action.

Finally, and perhaps most centrally, letting our imaginations run a little wild changes what we think is possible. Play can give us practice in changing the rules and the roles. It can give us a small space, like a blanket fort or a little poem, through which we can get a foretaste of another world.

Whereas work may often feel like the governing center of our everyday lives, Psalm 104 paints a picture of a world in which God's concern and care hold everything up. The Psalter invites us to sing to God,

> You set the earth on its foundations,
> so that it shall never be shaken. (Ps 104:5)

The poet goes on to describe a world in which God has created an order by setting boundaries (Ps 104:6–9).

This framing offers an alternative vision of work and generativity. The poet underlines the rhythms of creation, with the moon marking the seasons and the sun day and night (Ps 104:19–20). The psalmist sings that when the sun rises:

> People go out to their work
> and to their labor until the evening. (Ps 104:23)

The night shift, however, is left to the creatures of the forest and the lions (Ps 104:21–22).[148] This places our days and our labor *within* the broader scope of creation. We are guided by its rhythms and we share our habitats with others.

The driving force of creation is the generosity and sustenance that comes from God, rather than the effort of self-made men, prudent managers, or job creators. The poet offers up thanksgiving to God, declaring:

> From your lofty abode you water the mountains;
> the earth is satisfied with the fruit of your work. (Ps 104:13)

We are recipients of God's goodness, along with the rest of creation. The world is a commonwealth given by God for all, not a portfolio of private property possessed by a few. As the Psalter sings,

> You cause the grass to grow for the cattle,
> and plants for human cultivation. (Ps 104:14)[149]

In addition to sustenance, God brings forth a joyful and sacramental bounty. The poet praises God, who brings forth

> wine to gladden the human heart,
> oil to make the face shine
> and bread to strengthen the human heart. (Ps 104:15)

Even John Calvin, with his anxieties about human depravity, underlines the joyful vision that follows from this prayer.[150] In his commentary on Psalm 104, Calvin counsels that we are taught that God provides not only what is sufficient "for the ordinary purposes of life, but that in [God's] goodness he deals still more bountifully with [humans] by cheering their hearts with wine." Perhaps getting caught up in the play of the psalm, he goes on to write that it is "lawful to use wine not only in cases of necessity, but also thereby to make us merry." Not one to let too much "mirth" run amok, Calvin tempers this joy by placing it within a wider context of simplicity and interdependence. He notes that we should be careful with abundance, underlining that it must be shared and that it should sustain rather than oppress us.[151]

In his efforts to orient his community in sixteenth-century Geneva to the sufficiency and joy of creation and the Creator, Calvin sought to bring the Psalms and prayer into the center of people's shared lives.[152] He recommended that everyone engage in practices of prayer throughout the day in a modified version of the monastic hours. Only rather than following a clock, he proposed that prayer should be woven into our creaturely rhythms of daily life, serving as a constant and subtle tutor for our roles as receivers of grace and goodness. He wrote that we should pray "when we arise in the morning, before we begin our daily work, when we sit down to a meal, when by God's blessing we have eaten, when we are getting ready to retire."[153]

Calvin collaborated with others to compile the Geneva Psalter, which set the Psalms to metrical French with new tunes "composed not for choirs but for the whole congregation." This Psalter was used widely in churches *and* in homes. Calvin wanted the Psalms to be sung in houses and fields. He even went so far as to try and close the taverns in Geneva, and open Christian public houses where "food and wine were sold on a nonprofit basis" and "psalm singing was strongly encouraged." Such efforts to confine the gladness of the human heart were short lived. But the singing of the Psalms was not. In shared worship the power, poetry, creativity, and play of the Psalms invited people into the collaborative activity of lifting up their voices in joy. Children often led the way in this practice, as they taught the adults the new songs.[154]

Sometimes when I play with my son, we do not talk in full sentences. We wrestle and laugh. We repeat each other's nonsense phrases or imitate various bodily functions with our mouths. I call this our "brainstem time."

Spending so much of my days in my head, it is sheer joy just to be silly. Sometimes this romping play is simply a way to blow off some steam so that the pressure cooker does not explode, or it is a brief reprieve from other more pressing stressors and worries. I wonder, however, if there is not another kind of power hiding here.

There is an opening in silliness that is easy to look past, given so many cultural norms. Ahmed notes that the word *silliness*, etymologically, "comes from the word *sael*, originally meaning blessed, happy, or blissful. The word mutates over time; from blessed to pious, to innocent, to harmless, to pitiable, to weak and feeble."[155] To *spend* our time being silly is to be unproductive, to cut ourselves off from the structures and practices of value and power. And yet, if we were to dwell in this space where we cast off our normal roles and act childishly, we might find an opening through which we can see the blessings that surround us in creation.

The attention and passion cultivated by prayer might, furthermore, be one way to transform these practices of play from being feeble and fleeting breaks from the norm, into being formative moments that shape our hearts. Psalm 104 concludes by underlining the sacred character of rejoicing in creation. The psalm imagines creation as the call and response of rejoicing between God and creatures. The prayer of the poet calls on God to rejoice in God's works and hopes that the meditations of the psalm itself can be pleasing to God (Ps 104:31, 34). The poet, in turn, declares, "I will sing to the LORD as long as I live" (Ps 104:33). The psalm itself attempts to carry out this exercise in joy, singing to and seeking the rejoicing of the Creator.[156]

The dominant work ethic that guides so much of our days calls on us to engage in more serious work. Its norms and processes direct our action to privatized short-term productivity. It encourages us to act as managers over our emotions and children. It lures us into fitting our hopes into its spreadsheets and strategic plans. Such an ethic has found itself at odds with the transformation that is needed to begin to heal creation and our communities.

Psalm 104 directs us to have a different vision of the world and our place in it.[157] On the poet's account, the world is given as a communal blessing, rather than as private property. The psalmist groups all creatures together, singing:

> These all look to you
> to give them their food in due season;
> when you give to them, they gather it up

when you open your hand, they are filled with good things. (Ps 104:27–28)

This image of openhanded and vulnerable, intimate dependence is deepened as the poet continues to note that without the breath of God all creatures "die and return to dust." But when God sends God's spirit, God's breath, "they are created" and the ground is renewed (Ps 104:29–30).

We are not managers, but we are creatures. We can know this tactilely, practically, and imaginatively when we get on our knees—making ourselves child-sized to enter a blanket fort, to marvel at ants, or to kneel in prayer. By bending down to get closer to the ground, we can feel our interdependence with and proximity to the humus. We can slow down and breathe more deeply, knowing that our every breath comes from God, and that it was given so that we can rejoice, play, pray, and labor for a different world—a world that has always already been on the move. At first, this may seem silly, but in time we will see that it is one path to blessing.

10—Sowing the Seeds of Change in Social Spaces

Psalm 133

OUR HOUSEHOLD IS A multigenerational one. Several years ago my wife, my son, and I sold our single-family house and one of our two cars and moved in with my sister, my nephew, and my mother. Given our professional-class backgrounds—and the accompanying happiness scripts that associate maturity, freedom, success, and security with owning our own house—it took several intersecting personal crises to give us the courage to do so. I found myself burned out from work, both my wife and I were mourning the loss of three parents over the course of a year, and we were adjusting to life as parents ourselves after having been through the struggles of infertility. These personal trials intersected with our growing understanding of the ecological crisis and systemic injustice. Knowing that things had to change, personally and systemically, we sought to root this transformation in spaces of love and care.

While we do have a bit less living space and privacy, living together means that care is not spread quite so thinly. Our larger cultural practice of putting new parents, the two people who likely know the least about caring for a baby, in a house on their own is a bit strange. The strains that this model places on time and money are intense. Living together in a multifamily household has meant that the relationships of love and care that surround Teddy are thicker and denser. In a world of full schedules, shared space makes a spontaneous meal or a passing conversation possible. In the face of a crisis or even just a rough day, there are more people to step in and step up.

I am lifting up our efforts to create a shared household in this final meditation not because I think that it is a blueprint that you should or could apply in your context. This little experiment of ours is one that is largely about the specific blessings of our lives. I bring it up as *one* example of how we can begin to carry forward the work of social change needed to address climate change. Mainstream environmentalism often concludes its educational efforts by recommending some easy shifts in our consumer choices. Yet there is often nothing easy about these changes, as they require that we constantly choose something that goes against the dominant default. Furthermore, because these "choices" are in tension with concrete structures and powerful happiness scripts, the individual engaging in these environmental activities is often viewed as an irritant or breeds a sense of alienation. Rather than build a movement or even a community, these individual actions do nothing to change wider structures and cultural formations.

If we are to sustain our efforts *and* build collective power to bring about larger change, I think we would be better served by putting our energy into cultivating social practices and experimental spaces.[158] A social practice is something with repetition built into it, where the activity is shared with others, and its ongoing enactment builds a capacity and strength. Planting the seeds of change in social practices and spaces is an organic act that is quite similar to planting a tree—which could be seen as an extremely low-cost carbon capture machine that largely maintains itself and gains in strength when cultivated with others, or a tree could be seen as a creature who is worthy of our care and whose genius we are dependent upon.

Measured in terms of our carbon footprint, when we combined our households we did impact energy use and food waste. Though easier to measure, these impacts are relatively minor in comparison to what this communal shift has made possible socially. Sharing a house has simplified some of our bills and opened up time for other efforts—like resting, parenting, writing, showing up for movements, and cultivating alternative communities. Most importantly, care and love are not scarce resources, but they are undiminishable goods that grow in abundance as they are given energy and attention. They hold a power that can open our imaginations and sustain us in our wider efforts. Living in and being shaped by this common life cultivates a sense of trust that we can find sustenance and security not just in exchanging our labor for a wage, but also in simplifying and sharing. Life together gives us both a little breathing room from the dominant happiness scripts of the wicked and offers us a glimpse of what a different life can look like.[159]

While it is filled with gifts, life in community is also sometimes messy and difficult. Though the accumulation of care is often more exponential than additive, the more people there are to offer care also means that there are more people who need care. Common life makes relationships more complex, as you are no longer able to just put your best face on when you are with others. We bring our brokenness into the communities that we join and cultivate. It is not just as if this brokenness is something that I accidently track into our house when I have been outside. Rather, because intergenerational moral injury and trauma have shaped my heart and even the concrete exploitative and extractive architecture that I live in, this darkness dwells within our community. While community can be a space of healing, it is also one of struggle and conflict.[160]

The brokenness that we find in community, however, is not something that is incidental to the work that needs to be done to heal the earth. Rather, it is a manifestation of the very problems we face, and at a scale where we can begin to gain understanding and build capacities for healing and transformation. To begin to respond to the ecological crisis, we need to engage in social practices and find places of refuge and reorientation. Through this shared work we need to build our capacity to deal with emotions and realities that we often disavow, to understand the happiness scripts and habituated forms of everyday life that are embedded in unjust structures, and to begin to cultivate communal power and social imaginaries that will allow us to transform our ways of life to be joyful and just.

There are so many spaces where we might find this. One place to start could be at home with our children in the midst of the practices of parenting—as we explore God's creation, cry together, care for one another in the everyday, tell stories, enact happiness scripts, pray for forgiveness, celebrate holidays, and play. From here we could reach out to other parents, to neighbors, to members of our faith communities, to people in our extended family, to the wider proverbial village, so that we can begin the long, hard, and difficult work of healing and transforming our world.[161] This will all take a good deal of time, patience, and effort. It would have been nice if we had all started these experiments a long time ago, but as the proverb goes, the second best time to plant a tree is today.

Psalm 133 directs our prayers and hopes toward the blessings of life-giving community. This short song opens by declaring,

> How very good and pleasant it is
> when kindred live together in unity! (Ps 133:1)

The judgement of "very good" echoes the divine response of the opening chapters of Genesis that are spoken to the well-ordered creation and the shaping of the first community between men, women, and creation (Gen 1:31). The image here lifts up something beautiful that can animate our hearts and hands.[162]

The place of common life that the psalmist may have been seeking to evoke was the piece of land that was passed down through a family, which was a central part of the covenant with God. This land would not have been divided between households, but it would have been a shared grazing space and farmland.[163] When kindred live together in this way, there are more hands to help when the harvest comes, or when the terraced hills that house the grapevines and olive trees need to be repaired. There is also a sense that we do not own the land but it is a commonwealth, whose goodness comes from God, whose fruits are shared with gladness, and whose health needs to be maintained for future generations. This prayer points to the power of partnership and sharing that is rooted in right relationship between God, neighbor, and land.

In this pregnant image of common and cooperative life the psalmist evokes an entire library's worth of lived lessons. As Cassiodorus writes, this line works in the way of "a demonstrator rather than a speaker." It teaches through the gesture of "the extended finger rather than continuous speech." We are pointed to the kind of formation that comes from following the example of others. Or more precisely, the training we gain in community does not just come from watching or looking up to others, but we find encouragement through *shared* examples. In community we can find that we are motivated and energized by delight and beauty, that we are ignited by "the fire of mutual love."[164]

Yet, before I get too caught up in the beauty and allure of this image, it is also important that it remain concrete and realistic. Dietrich Bonhoeffer opens his book on Christian communal life with this very verse. He underlines the joy and the blessing that comes from a common life of shared prayer. Yet, he is also careful to note that one of the great obstacles to such a life together is "a wishful image." The counsel here is that we should not enter community with demands about what others must do, but that we should be oriented by the practice of thankfully receiving. This practice of gratitude does not require that we accept things as they are, but rather it points us toward a spirit of generosity that fosters a nurturing space where people are able to grow and transform together.[165]

The psalmist continues by evoking another powerful image, saying that

> It is like the precious oil on the head,
> running down upon the beard,
> on the beard of Aaron,
> running down over the collar of his robes. (Ps 133:2)

The image of oil running down through one's hair calls to mind a context of festive celebration and hospitality. This was an experience that does even more than paint a picture in the mind's eye. This cultural practice activates other senses, as it would be something that we could feel washing over our bodies, like the sensation of being covered with warm water in a shower. The oil also calls to mind powerful memories of smell that mark the occasion of a family gathering together in celebration. This might be like the smell of your grandmother's house or of grilled food on a summer's day. This poetic line seeks to play upon the magical aura of well-being and communion that accompanies celebration.[166]

The oil of this initial association quickly flows over and unites with another charged context, that of the anointing of Aaron and priests. The fluidity of these two images brings together the goodness of community with the practice of anointing those who are called to carry out God's purposes of restoration and new creation. Jerome, preaching to his brothers in common life in the shadow of the nativity in Bethlehem, connects this anointing to Christ (which in Greek simply means "the anointed one"). Christ, on this account, is anointed so that he may also anoint us to "love justice and hate wickedness."[167] The community that provides blessing is also one that is anointed for a purpose in the wider world.

In just a couple of lines, the psalmist has called to mind the power of communal care and prayer, and has directed us toward cooperating in joy for the sake of a greater justice. Yet, these culturally charged images of familial and priestly life are also marked by obstacles. The rules and structures that give shape to family life are often premised upon the exploitation of other peoples and they lead to an inward-looking concern that disregards others. Erich Zenger notes that while Psalm 133 draws on images that might be associated with elite festival culture, it evokes a joyful "philosophy of life" that is only realized in a comprehensive fellowship "which excludes no one." Furthermore, too often we imagine that the religious world and the spiritual life is one that is compartmentalized and divided off. The image of the priest might leave us with the sense that prayer is something done in holy spaces and in solitude. Gustavo Gutierrez, however, cites Psalm 133 in full in a discussion of the proper pursuit of spiritual solitude. He differentiates between an individualism that sees the presence of others as an interruption to spiritual practice, with a solitude that cultivates a passion for deep and just community.[168]

In light of these obstacles, Isasi-Diaz's formulation of the "kin-dom of God" might be helpful. She offers this as an alternative to the cultural imaginaries that accompany the term "kingdom of God"—which appeals to the feudal political structures of kings, which are chronologically and practically distant from our daily lives and that are steeped in practices of patriarchy and oppression. Kin-dom frames the call to discipleship with an image and context that is rooted in the core of our lives—the space of kinship and family. Specifically, she proposes that we come to understand and incarnate our communal ideals by learning from the acts of love, care, and survival practiced by Latinx families, and especially women, in contexts of oppression and exploitation.[169] Psalm 133, similarly, draws our attention to spaces of common life and commonwealth where mutual care and love show us ways of living steeped in joy and anointed for the work of justice.

When we combined our households, Carly and I had all kinds of visions of a world set apart. We imagined that we would be gardening together during the day, playing games in the evenings with the kids, and discussing books when they went to bed. While all of these things have been a part of our common life, it has consistently been a struggle to find the time and energy to do them. Even with this shared space it is often difficult to be in the same place, at the same time, with enough energy to deeply engage one another.

In an effort to cultivate better communication, a couple of years into the experiment, we designated Monday evenings as a time for a family meeting. Initially we ran this a bit like a committee, which is not to say that we followed Robert's Rules of Order. Luckily, I never had to hear my son say, "I would like to call the question on the debate on the current motion regarding the shoe rack by the door." We did, however, keep an agenda and take turns playing the role of facilitator. My wife and my sister Becky devised a structure that would help frame our conversations so that they were not simply an airing of grievances. We began the meetings sharing our gratitude for what others had recently done (focusing on lifting up the kids) and ended by talking about something we were looking forward to.

After holding our meetings like this for about a year, my sister noted that this structure was not quite cultivating the communication or the community for which we were looking. She proposed that the committee-like form was giving us committee-like content. Managerial or bureaucratic practices activate people in specific ways and cultivate specific kinds of relationships. While these can sometimes be helpful in talking over a contentious issue, they might not be the best forms to grow common life. She proposed that we spend our Monday evenings doing something together that was more joyful, and that would exercise a different part of our selves and different aspects of our relationships.

Whatever social practices or shared spaces we seek to cultivate moving forward will likely be marked by compromise and struggle. Our ideal images will often be obstacles for real relationship just as much as they are motivating guides. Our efforts at communicating and simply being together will continue to be shaped by the broken inheritance and structures that have shaped us. Doing something different is difficult. It takes patience, but even more it takes collaboration and cooperation—capacities that we probably have not exercised enough in our lives. Because so many of our communal and cultural defaults turn us in the wrong direction, we will need to be very intentional about the kinds of communities that we cultivate.

In my darker moments, when I think about Teddy's future, I wonder if these hopeful efforts are misguided. Part of me wonders—given everything I know about how dire things look for the coming decades and with how vast and systemic these challenges are—if I should be doing everything that I can to accumulate money so that he can be on the other side of the fence in the coming eco-apocalypse. At the least, perhaps I should be toughening him up for what is going to be a harsh world.

But when I have had a moment to breathe and when I am grounded in common life, I am convinced that the opposite is true. I could busy myself with trying to help him succeed in the games of a world that is ostensibly breaking down. Yet, even in the most self-concerned terms, these efforts would probably be like having spent my youth learning the trade of VCR repair. The best thing I can do for him is to help him learn how to live with the power of creation—learning to share common life with others, to co-operate for the common good, to trust love, to make peace, to cultivate joy, and to listen to his fellow creatures. If there is hope for the future or criteria for resilience on an imperiled planet, surely is it grounded in the collective power that comes from the care of creatures, creation, and the Creator.

Psalm 133 concludes by lifting up the power of creation, cooperation, and peace. The poet sings that the life of goodness and peace, "is like the dew of Hermon, / which falls on the mountains of Zion" (Ps 133:3). For farmers in ancient Israel, who relied on the rains rather than the abundance of rivers, the daily gift of dew was a constant reminder of one's dependence upon the Creator and of one's interdependent and participatory place in creation. The two mountains evoked by the psalmist, Hermon and Zion, mark northern and southern peaks, and indicate a shared unity. As William Brown notes, "These geographically extreme points share mountain dew, as it were, and thus common ground." The image evoked here is like Woody Guthrie's song about the commonwealth of the United States stretching

> From California to the New York island
> From the redwood forest to the Gulf Stream waters.

This is an image of political peace built on a fuller experience of peace, of shalom, known from a life of shared sustenance and joy.[170]

As we begin to think about how we will work for justice and peace in the face of climate catastrophe, the Psalter provides some direction. It shows us a poetic path where our covenant with God is intertwined with our cooperation with our fellow creatures and creation. The power of God and the work of justice flow like the oil of celebration and the dew of sustenance through these common spaces of care, sharing, simplicity, prayer, and peace. The psalm anoints us with these oils and waters to attend to spaces and labors that our accounting schemes understand as externalities and that our cultural conventions compartmentalize as private, interior, or ephemeral. The Psalter directs us to see the potency of the space of spirit, silence, sabbath, and prayer. We are guided to see the power of the common life we share with children, family, and friends. To cultivate justice we will need to pursue healing, penance, redemption, and forgiveness here. We will also need to nurture these spaces through joy, stories, play, and celebration.

The poet concludes by declaring,

For *there* the Lord ordained his blessing,
life forevermore. (Ps 133:3b)

We find the blessing of God in the midst of everyday life, in community, on the land, in festival joy, in our acts of faithful service, and in the harmony of peace.[171]

As we look for *where* God's blessing might be in our midst, or how we might participate in cultivating the common good, perhaps we should look for the pointed finger of the demonstrator gesturing to social spaces. Though so much has been privatized and emptied out in our time, we can still find little openings of social infrastructure all around us. Schools, playgrounds, corner diners, parks, pools, sidewalks, libraries, barber shops, grocery stores, public houses (which is to say pubs), and athletic fields, among others, are places where people can connect, collaborate, support, and share.[172] While many of these spaces have been constructed to direct us toward isolated consumption or competition, they can be transformed.

Chief among these social spaces, which hide in plain sight and hold the seeds for change, are churches. In the United States there are countless buildings and plots of land that are communally held. Rather than serving as chapels of comfort, conformity, or escape, these communities could combine Scripture, spiritual practice, popular pedagogies, festival life, and intergenerational relationships to transform our lives and build our capacity for the work of justice and joy.[173]

In our efforts to cultivate the social change demanded by climate change and systemic injustice, perhaps we would be well served by looking to the social experiments initiated by Christian communities in so many different contexts and centuries. Perhaps we could expand our sense of what is possible and beautiful by looking to the community of artists, priests, peasants, and revolutionaries initiated by Ernesto Cardenal, which sought to create a different kind of common life on the Island of Solentiname in Nicaragua. We might find inspiration from the Beguines movements in late medieval Europe, where women created alternative communities of common life on the margins of the church and city—sharing a life of simplicity and prayer that empowered them to care for the sick and the poor. In both these cases and so many others, the communal singing and reading of the Psalms served to sustain their spirits and to transform their imaginations.[174]

By looking to wider spaces, learning from movements and experiments, and meditating on the wisdom of Scripture, we can begin to see with greater clarity how the intimate acts of caring for our children and making kin can fit into the work of deep and sustaining transformation. Through prayer we can train our attention on the power that is flowing all around us.

Late in the afternoon one day, I am working in my office at home. I am trying to finish up writing a section. Hanging over my head are unanswered emails, a report that needs to be submitted, and so many other little tasks. I feel not just tired but also something else. It is less than despairing and demoralized, but more than anxious. Perhaps I am feeling all of those things, and I am simply in the state that exists in between as it disavows larger questions and concerns while seeking to push through its to-do list. None the less, I continue white-knuckling the task at hand in hopes of accomplishing . . . something.

Through the door I hear Teddy and my nephew, Logan, calling. It is Monday. Tonight we are going to work in the garden together. At first I find myself a little irritated with their interruption as my concentration has been broken. I am reminded of a joke: What is a theologian? An old man sitting *alone* in a room writing about love. I look around and my windows are drawn shut and my door is closed.

Instead of powering through on my own, I answer the call. I close my computer and open the door. These tasks will be waiting for me tomorrow, and perhaps then, I will have the spirit and power to approach them differently.

As I go outside, I am welcomed by a beautiful spring day. The bugs and oppressive heat have not yet claimed our yard. I join our household as we weed the strawberries and uncover a patch of plants that we thought had failed to get established last year. This season they are blooming forth with new life. While we were not watching they sent out runners and their roots grew deeper. Teddy and Logan again call me away from these labors to play. For a moment, I pretend with them that we are on a spaceship and on the run.

How good and lovely it is when kindred dwell together. It is in these spaces that we can begin to live into the tasks of new creation for which we have been anointed and in which we can find the daily dew of God that will sustain us. Here God's blessing dwells and it extends out to the ends of the earth.

My wife calls down the yard to us to say that it is time for dinner. Teddy takes my hand as we walk toward the house and I am reminded that there is another way to face our shared future. I have been trained to sing old songs about work and productivity, yet I am reminded that there are new songs that we can learn to sing together. While I remain a slow learner, the Psalms and my son are patiently teaching me.

Endnotes

1. For a complex account on the layers of denial related to climate change, see Norgaard, *Living in Denial*.
2. Kaufman, "Carbon Footprint Sham."
3. For a critique of an approach of eco-consumerism or eco-business see, for example, Dauvergne, *Environmentalism of the Rich*; Dickinson, *Green Good News*, 61–65.
4. For an overview of the rebound effect, see Rowson, *New Agenda*, 41–45. On how the issue is not primarily consumption but production and the production of desire, see Rieger, *Theology in the Capitalocene*, 36–42; *No Rising Tide*, 101–6. Whereas I am emphasizing agency exercised in the sphere of social reproduction, Rieger importantly underlines the transformation in the spheres of production and the Christian traditions that could help inspire this (106–16).
5. John Cassian, *Conferences* 11.4–5/ Cassian, *Conferences*, 384–85.
6. Michel Foucault gives a helpful account of this form of pastoral power that connects it to a long history of Christian pastoral formations and more recent regimes of governmentality, which cuts across divisions often drawn between religion and politics and situates disciplines, counter-conduct, and everyday practices on the same plane as spiritual exercises. Foucault, *Security, Territory, Population*. For Foucault's understanding of power and the agency this understanding opens in everyday life see Tran, "Otherness of Children," 191–203; *Foucault and Theology*, 44–47; 115–24. See also Dickinson, *Exercises in New Creation*, 56–60.
7. Norgaard, *Living in Denial*, 61, 73–74.
8. While I am drawing on Walter Brueggemann's account of the function of the Psalms as reorienting, I am not following the typological functions of orientation, disorientation, and reorientation that he proposes in any strict sense. See Brueggemann, *Psalms and the Life*, 10–15; *Praying the Psalms*, 1–15.
9. Herbert, "Twenty-Third Psalm," 20.
10. Schaefer, *Psalms*, 58–59.
11. The sufficiency and simplicity described here is not a separate peace that is cultivated by those who can afford a different kind of lifestyle. Rather it is part of the mosaic of a social imaginary that can serve as the basis of political education, grassroots power, and solidarity. For a theological vision of sufficiency, see Blosser, "And It Was Good." For a Christian spirituality of simplicity, see Foster, *Freedom of Simplicity*.
12. Alter, *Book of Psalms*, 78n3.

13. On alternative possibilities for more collective forms of organization and leadership see, for example, Lewis et al., *Another Way*; Salvatierra and Heltzel, *Faith-Rooted Organizing*; Conder and Rhodes, *Organizing Church*. On ways that political demonstrations can help shape new subjectivities and communities centered on cooperation and care, see Day, *Religious Resistance to Neoliberalism*, 131–86; Quintana, *Politics of Bodies*, ch. 5.

14. For a wide-ranging and life-giving collection of perspectives on sustaining climate activism, see Schade and Jonas, eds., *Rooted and Rising*.

15. For her account of a popular hermeneutics and a reading of Psalm 137 from the perspective of Cuban American exile, see Isasi-Diaz, *Mujerista Theology*, ch. 3. To see Psalm 23 from the perspective of the poor, oppressed, and marginalized, consult Claudio Carvalhaes's ten contemporary renderings of the psalm in *Liturgies form Below*, part 4.

16. On the public and political relevance of practical theological reflection on everyday acts of parenting and care and centering the marginalized voices of children, see Miller-McLemore, "Children and Religion."

17. Nabhan and Trimble, *Geography of Childhood*, 5.

18. Alston, ed., *We Speak for Ourselves*, 103; Baker-Fletcher, *Sisters of Dust*, 1–6. For an environmental justice reading of the Gospels, see Dickinson, *Green Good News*.

19. Saverin, "Thoreau of the Suburbs." For the limits of romantic visions of wilderness and white environmental imaginaries see Dickinson, *Exercises in New Creation*, 11–13; 80–87; 163–66; 261–65; *Green Good News*, 8–12; 43–44; 75–76; 156–59.

20. Interpreters have long reduced the phrase "all the earth" to refer to only humans—ranging from Cassiodorus's statement that this is clearly an allegory and that it refers to "man rather than soil" to modern German biblical scholars' reduction of the phrase to referring either to the people of Israel or all nations. Cassiodorus, *Expositio psalmarum* 99.2/ Cassiodorus, *Explanation of the Psalms*, vol. 2, 444; Hossfeld and Zenger, *Psalms 2*, 492. I follow Arthur Walker-Jones in his wider reading of this phrase. *Green Psalter*, 92, 107. More broadly, I find the assumed categories that underly these aforementioned interpretations—the distinction between the spiritual and the material; the compartmentalization of religion, politics, and nature; and the division drawn between redemption and creation—to be both unsuited for biblical imaginaries and problematic for contemporary constructive readings. I tend to read the poetry of the Psalter in more dynamic, holistic, connective, creative, and creational terms.

21. Davis, *Scripture, Culture, and Agriculture*, 29. The NRSV has changed the translation to "serve."

22. The Greek term (*douleuō*) in the Gospel of Matthew is the same as the one in the Greek translation of the psalm.

23. Mays, "Worship, World, and Power," 321.

24. Schaefer, *Psalms*, 262. For an account of how this covenantal declaration fits into a universal expansion of the covenant with God see Lohfink and Zenger, *God of Israel*, ch. 6. They see this as part of a shift in understanding of the covenant relationship and the question of salvation *from* being about the soul's admission into another world *to* the question, will "harmonious songs of praise" ever sound again "from all of creation?" Or further, "whether in the desecrated and empty spaces of the world

Endnotes

God's honor can be present again" (196–97).

25. On the tension between a neoliberal view of nature as a natural resource, and a soteriological and eschatological vision of creation see Clapp, *Naming Neoliberalism*, ch. 6. On the embodied and practical pedagogy of Christ, see Dickinson, *Green Good News*, ch 4. See further on the lilies and the birds sayings, Dickinson, *Exercises in New Creation*, 239–51. See also Rubem Alves's gloss on the children of the kingdom saying pointing toward a revolutionary imagination. *Tomorrow's Child*, 98–99.

26. For an approach to ecological theology and practice grounded in the web of relationships in a watershed, see Myers, ed., *Watershed Discipleship*.

27 On the historical and systemic assault on cooperation and the enclosure of the commons, and a theological account of alternative forms of social life, see Eberhart, *Rooted and Grounded*, esp. chs. 1 and 4.

28. On the emergence of these norms, their relationship to everyday life, and structures, see Shove, *Comfort, Cleanliness, and Convivence*.

29. Soelle, *Suffering*, 36–39.

30. Brueggemann, *Praying the Psalms*, 7–8.

31. Rashi, *Commentary on Psalms*, 221.

32. Brueggemann, *Psalms and the Life of Faith*, 11–13.

33. Cited in Brueggemann and Bellinger, *Psalms*, 78–79.

34. Katongole, *Born from Lament*, 110. Brueggemann, *Psalms and the Life of Faith*, 21.

35. Augustine, *Enarrationes in Psalmos* 12.3/Augustine, *Expositions of the Psalms 1–32*, 173.

36. On the social, structural, and creational horizons for Augustine's critique of the flesh, see Dickinson, *Exercises in New Creation*, 170–78.

37. Clifford, *Psalms 1–72*.

38. Townes, *Breaking the Fine Rain of Death*, 24. On the connection of communal lament and the power of hope centered on justice and joy, see 175–86.

39. For a theological account of these dynamics of vulnerability in life before God see Culp, *Vulnerability and Glory*. For a theological anthropology of vulnerability from the perspective of maternity, see Gandolfo, *Power and Vulnerability of Love*.

40. Ellen Davis proposes that this shift is often made through simply breaking the silence or by God offering healing in unexpected ways. *Getting Involved with God*, 20–21.

41. Tina Miller notes that in normative discourses that male paternal care is typically spoken of as "involvement" rather than nurture, because of the latter's association with breastfeeding. Yet these ideas of involvement are wide-ranging and can sometimes be limited to providing economically. *Making Sense of Fatherhood*, 5, 17. John Wall helpfully names the link of this gender role with notions of generativity, and counters a softer patriarchy of disciplinary male involvement with a child-oriented approach centered on mutuality that can loosen up some of these gendered strictures. *Ethics in Light of Childhood*, 156–60.

42. Cardenal, *Psalms*, 15. Ironically, Cardenal would go on to be a member of cabinet, serving as the minister of culture in Nicaragua from 1979 to 1987.

43. Chrysostom, *Commentary*, 2:199.

44. Chrysostom, *Commentary*, 2:200.

45. For my treatment of spiritual exercises and how they build relational capacities, see Dickinson, *Exercises in New Creation*, esp. ch 5. For a theological account of how saying grace can unfold into the fullness of life, see Wirzba, *Food and Faith*, 179–210.

46. Miller-McLemore, *In the Midst of Chaos*, 1–20. See also Gustavo Gutierrez's critique of elitist and individualistic Christian spiritual traditions that separate the life of faith from everyday concerns. He helpfully contextualizes these tendencies against a backdrop of dispossession from the land and structures of exploitation and extraction, and points toward the alternative power of the spiritualities of people's movements and a transformed relationship with past traditions. *We Drink from Our Own Wells*, 9–18.

47. On issues of ambiguity in the manuscript tradition and an account of interpreting the psalm as either written by or from the perspective of a mother, see Knowles, "Woman at Prayer."

48. For an account of this dynamic of externalizing, exploiting, and extracting from acts of care and the formation of the nuclear family and the domestic sphere as a central part of processes of colonialism and capitalism, and not some kind of anthropological given, see Patel and Moore, *History of the World*, ch. 4. For a theological account of the class, gender, and racial dynamics of household care labor, see Joh, "Relating to Household Labor Justly."

49. Fraser and Jaeggi, *Capitalism*, 31.

50. Peterson, *Everyday Ethics*.

51. Fraser, "Contradictions of Capital and Care." For a global account of these movements see Federici, *Re-Enchanting the World*, 86–89, 124–30, 137–43, 188–96. For an account of how the industrial working class was recycled into care industries in the United States, see Winant, *Next Shift*. For an account that links these revolutionary agencies along lines of reproduction and production understood democratically and ecologically, and that calls on theologians to immerse themselves in these spaces, see Rieger, *Theology in the Capitalocene*, 48–54, 81–87.

52. Hebblethwaite and Kavanagh, *Our Two Gardens*.

53. Klein, *This Changes Everything*.

54. On the formative character of children's stories, see Miller-McLemore, *In the Midst of Chaos*, 161–173. On the formative practices of reading and writing more broadly, see Dickinson, *Exercises in New Creation*.

55. Brueggemann and Bellinger, *Psalms*, 83.

56. Walker-Jones, *Green Psalter*, 22–24.

57. Miller, *Interpreting the Psalms*, 95.

58. Brueggemann, *Psalms and the Life of Faith*, 224–25.

59. On the interrelated web of the power of stories, their instantiation in cultural production, and their power in everyday and institutional contexts see Emilie Townes's account of the "fantastic hegemonic imagination." *Womanist Ethics*, esp. 18–22. Townes proposes (164) that we dismantle these structures of evil by beginning in the "everydayness of moral acts" and concludes this book with poetic verse on what this looks like that deeply resonates with this psalm.

60. On the tension between the animating story of the neoliberal intensification of the American Dream and Christian stories of sufficiency and neighbor love, see Blosser,

"And It Was Good."

61. For this description of midrash, see Gafney, *Womanist Midrash*, 3–4.

62. Braude, ed., *Midrash on Psalms*, 1:189.

63. On the covenantal commons and the critique of the economy of empire in a trajectory from the Law, through the prophets, and onto the Gospels, see Dickinson, *Green Good News*, esp., 57–61, 65–74, 77–84.

64. Basil, *Homilia* 14b.1/Basil, *On Social Justice*, 91.

65. Basil *Homilia* 14b.2.

66. Basil, *Homilia* 6.7.

67. Basil, *Homilia* 14b.3.

68. Basil, *Homilia* 14a.6, quoted in Holman, *Hungry Are Dying*, 112–13.

69. Basil *Homilia* 6.1–3; 7.1; 8.8.

70. Nagara, *A is for Activist*.

71. Townes, *Womanist Ethics*, viii–xi.

72. On the Christian position of praying this psalm in between perfection and the need for forgiveness, see Steussy, *Psalms*,107.

73. See, for example, Jennifer Harvey's account of "racial scripts" in *Raising White Kids*, 172–210.

74. Saad and Jones, "U.S. Concern"

75. On the "unmoved," see Rowson, *New Agenda*, 7.

76. On the ways professional class parents manage layers of anxiety, see Katz, "Just Managing."

77. Ahmed, *Promise of Happiness*, 59.

78. For a theological account of the intersectional issues tied up in the treatment of animals and a constructive vision of Black veganism, see Carter, *Spirit of Soul Food*, esp. chs. 3 and 4.

79. Calvin, *Commentary*, 2:17. The connotation of emulation is even stronger in the Greek and Latin translations of the psalm, Ambrose, *Explanatio Psalmorum/Commentary on Twelve Psalms*, 36.4.

80. Brown, *Seeing the Psalms*, 191.

81. On the move from resistance to re-existence, see Walsh, " Decolonial *For,*" 18.

82. Miranda, *Communism in the Bible*, 42.

83. Gillingham, *Psalms Through the Centuries.*

84. As Walter Brueggemann and William Bellinger note, the psalm is not so much a theory about the "universal structure of reality" as it is "a pragmatic homily on how to live in the face of the observation that the wicked prosper." *Psalms*, 183.

85. Luther, *Four Psalms of Comfort*, 225.

86. Luther, *Four Psalms of Comfort*, 219.

87. Ambrose, *Expl. Ps. (Commentary)* 36.3.

88. Ambrose, *Expl. Ps. (Commentary)* 35.7, 25.

89. Ambrose, *Expl. Ps. (Commentary)* 37.62.

90. On Ambrose and the commons of creation see, for example, Ambrose, "*De Nabuthae*

historia"/Ambrose, "Of Naboth," 1.1, 12.53.

91. Brown, *Seeing the Psalms*, 37.

92. While I am not using the term "professional class" in a strict sense, I am invoking Barbara and John Ehrenreich's account of the professional managerial class. They coined this term to demarcate a class of people whose task it is to manage the working class on behalf of the ruling class, but who do so with the goals and values of rationalizing and service rather than extracting profit. Yet, the Ehrenreichs note that decades of neoliberal hegemony have eroded the governing rationalities, values, and power of this class to the point of virtual collapse. Ehrenreich and Ehrenreich, *Death of a Yuppie Dream*.

93. Weintrobe, "Difficult Problem of Thinking," 39.

94. Cassiodorus, *Expositio psalmarum* 6.1, 6.11/Cassiodorus, *Explanation of the Psalms*, 1:90, 98.

95. Brown, *Seeing the Psalms*, 26–27, 38.

96. Joerg Rieger and Kwok Pui-lan connect this cry from the Psalter to a way of seeing beyond the false narrative of empire, approaching God "from the underside of history," and pursuing repentance, restitution, and forgiveness. *Occupy Religion*, 101.

97. Casey, *Athirst for God*, 127.

98. I do not have in mind here the sacramental observance of penance, though that may be relevant for some readers. I am thinking something that is more in the spirit of the early church's practice of penance that was done with a confidant or friends. For a historical account of the varying practices of penance in early and largely European Christian traditions, see McNeil, *History of the Cure of Souls*.

99. For an account of how meticulous methods of penance risk an overly scrupulous introversion, see McNeil, *Cure of Souls*, 160–61. For an account of how some of the disciplines and apparatuses of the earlier Christian pastoral tradition were transformed and redeployed in modern biopolitics that regulated individuated and normalized populations, see Foucault, *Security, Territory, Population*. For an extension of this line of thought into contemporary neoliberal formations, see Dardot and Laval, *New Way of the World*, esp. ch. 9, and Rogers-Vaughn, *Caring for Souls*.

100. Steussy, *Psalms*, 190–91.

101. Gregory the Great, *Dialogi* 3.34/Gregory the Great, *Dialogues*, 173.

102. This translation is from Alter, *Book of the Psalms*, 456.

103. Luther, *Seven Penitential Psalms*, 191.

104. Calvin, *Commentary on the Book of Psalms*, 5:133

105. On the processes of responsiblization see Brown, *Undoing the Demos*, 131–34.

106. Matthew Huber laments that in the face of "carbon guilt," professional-class people "rather than question the politics of privatism," double down "on a privatized political project of individual behavioral change." Huber, *Climate Change as Class War*, 156.

107. Blake, "London."

108. This psalm is likely even more familiar insofar as Stephen Reid characterizes the hymn "Joy to the World" as a rendition of Psalm 96. *Listening In*, 53.

109. Not only is this psalm itself ancient, but it also echoes or is echoed by several other

Endnotes

psalms and a version of it appears in 1 Chronicles 16:23–33.

110. This heading can be traced back to the Septuagint but is not in the Masoretic text.

111. Augustine, *Expositio in Psalmos* 95.1/Augustine, *Expositions of the Psalms, 73–98*, 423.

112. Augustine, *Expositio in Psalmos* 95.2.

113. Walker-Jones, *Green Psalter*, 91–93.

114. Walker-Jones, *Green Psalter*, 118. The imagery and poetry of declaring God as king is dangerous and slippery. Much of the history of Christian tradition could be regarded as stories about how empires tried to rebrand their old songs of domination and extraction as new songs of God's glory and justice. See, for example, Joerg Rieger's account of the imperial appropriations of Christ, and the theological surplus that exceeds such machinations, *Christ and Empire*. Augustine's triumphalist deployment of these very verses of Psalm 96, in the aforementioned sermon and even more so in *The City of God*, are prime examples. Augustine, *De civitate Dei*, 6.24. For a counterpoint that interprets the royal theology of the Psalter as a postexilic ideological criticism of imperial theologies, see Reid, "David."

115 On these valences of "firmly established," see Brown, *Seeing the Psalms*, 30. For "equity" see Alter, *Psalms*, 229.

116. Augustine, *Expositio in Psalmos* 95.2.

117. On the anxieties that animate so much of professional class parenting, see Katz, "Childhood as Spectacle."

118. On the disruption of happiness scripts and the role of the killjoy, see Ahmed, *Promise of Happiness*, esp. 64–79, 196.

119. Schaefer, *Psalms*, 239.

120. Walker-Jones, *The Green Psalter*, 180 no. 5.

121. On the logic of the Sabbath, see Dickinson, *Green Good News*, 65–73.

122. Carvalhaes, *Ritual at World's End*, 52. Carvalhaes's work illustrates how liturgy and ritual can be oriented toward communal practices that engage with our creatureliness, work for justice, and heal systems of exploitation and extraction.

123. On hope as a practice realized through rituals, and specifically through the everyday embodiment of motherhood, where love, care, and cooperation counter competition, isolation, and individualism, see Day, *Religious Resistance to Neoliberalism*, ch. 5. For a theological vision of how celebration can play a role in communal transformation see Goizueta, "Fiesta."

124. Gutierrez Aguilar, *Rhythms of the Pachakuti*, xxxix–xl.

125. Walker-Jones, *Green Psalter*, 178n18, 118.

126. On the ambivalence and often ascetic sensibilities of Christian spiritual traditions toward embodied, creational, and joyful beauty, and for the openings of a spirituality of beauty, see Jantzen, *Place of Springs*, esp. ch 3.

127. Katz, *Growing Up Global*, 95–96. See further her ethnographic account of Sudanese children's play with the hegemonic roles and debris of capitalism in ways that are inventive and subversive (95–108).

128. Alves, *Tomorrow's Child*, 90–91.

129. Alves, *Tomorrow's Child*, 93.

130. On the connection between liturgy and play, see Goto, *Grace of Playing*.

131. On Walter Benjamin's account of how the mimetic improvision of children—which is tactile, inventive, and which combines perception and praxis—is different from bourgeois education where people are taught to look without touching, parrot back the correct answer, solve problems internally, and sit passively, see Buck-Morss, *Dialectics of Seeing*, 263–65. She goes on to explore the potential Benjamin saw in the adult engagement with the world through child's play and fairy tale as a re-enchanting of the world for the purpose of social transformation and encountering nature as a commons (273–77).

132. The deeply active character of much of this poem's use of present participles is often lost in translation. Alter, *Psalms*, 362n2. One translation attempts to capture the ways that God moves, sends word, and works through air and fire, rendering the dynamic poetry: "Riding (is he) on the wings of the wind. / Making the wind his messengers, fire and flame his servants." Hossfeld and Zenger, *Psalms 3*, 43.

133. William Brown calls Psalm 104 the most extensive account of *creatio continua* in the Old Testament, *Seeing the Psalms*, 159.

134. Jerome, Ep. 46.11–12.

135. Jerome, *Homily* 31/Jerome, *Homilies*, 223, 228.

136. Brown, *Seven Pillars of Creation*, 146–147.

137. Walker-Jones underlines that humans are only mentioned in four verses of the psalm, indicating its ecological and more-than-human vision of creation. Walker-Jones, *Green Psalter*, 139, 140. Ernesto Cardenal's cosmic rendering of the psalm as the story of the evolution of life amplifies this by only mentioning humans in one line. Cardenal, *Psalms*, 7–12.

138. Fishbane, *Sacred Attunement*, 139.

139. For an account of the evolution of the work ethic and a characterization of this as a "work society," see Weeks, *Problem with Work*, ch. 1. For my own account of the neoliberal gospel of work in contrast to the healing work of Christ in the Gospels, see *Green Good News*, ch. 5. For a vision of how the constructive dimensions of labor can be combined with religion for social change and justice, see Rieger and Henkel-Rieger, *United We Are a Force*.

140. Weeks, *Problem with Work*, 70–76.

141. Illouz, *Saving the Modern Soul*, 103.

142. Illouz, *Cold Intimacies*, 24–36.

143. Katz, "Just Managing"; Foucault, *Birth of Biopolitics*, 226–30.

144. On the way that emotions are managed to fit norms in the face of climate change, see Norgaard, *Living in Denial*, ch. 4.

145. These formations of work cannot simply be countered by time with family, as many of the norms and structures that shape family life often go hand in glove with structures of racial capitalism. Weeks, *Problem with Work*, ch. 4. See further, Hall, *Conceiving Parenthood*; Winant, *Next Shift*, ch 4. In this book I have sought to work against romanticized notions of family as a haven set apart, and instead have crossed practices of care and prayer so as to transform the norms and structures of familial life and, in turn, wider social and political forms.

146. Miller-McLemore, *Also a Mother*, 153–55.

Endnotes

147. Peterson, *Everyday Ethics*, 82.

148. Brown, *Seven Pillars of Creation*, 147.

149. The phrase "human cultivation" is William Brown's translation. *Seven Pillars of Creation*, 142.

150. On Calvin's reading of the Psalms as a means of training our attention on delight and gratitude, see Culp, *Vulnerability and Glory*, 172–77.

151. Calvin, *Commentary*, 5:155–157.

152. On Calvin's readings of the Psalms as healing performances of prayer for traumatized peoples and communities, see Jones, *Trauma and Grace*, ch. 3.

153. Calvin, *Institutes of Christian Religion*, 3.20.50.

154. Boulton, *Life in God*, 33–44. Calvin, "Form of Prayers," 163–64.

155. Ahmed, *Promise of Happiness*, 220.

156. Brown, *Seven Pillars of Creation*, 150–51.

157. Psalm 104 is often aligned with new life and a different world in the Jewish liturgical calendar as it is "sung on the morning of Yom Kippur, as a pledge that new life will emerge out of penance and sorrow. It is chanted in the evening of the new moon, thus consecrating another month to God. It is recited from the Sabbath of the feast of Sukkoth to Passover (i.e., throughout the winter), in anticipation of new life in the Spring." Schaefer, *Psalms*, 258–59.

158. On social practices, experiments, and philosophical theology, see Dickinson, *Exercises in New Creation*, esp. ch 6. For a consideration of the social practices and spaces of community gardens and dinner churches, see Dickinson, *Green Good News*, 37–46, Ch 6. For an account of how experiments in food justice can lead to education, further engagement in social justice movements, and solidarity, see Ryan-Simpkins and Nogueira-Godsey, "Tangible Actions."

159. On the political importance of providing a foretaste of another world, see, for example, Rieger and Kwok, *Occupy Religion*, 5, 44, 122–27.

160. Dorothy Day often writes with profound honesty on the brokenness we bring into communal life and of the possibility of healing. See, for example, *Loaves and Fishes*, esp. 37–39. For resources on how white people in the United States can begin the work of reparation in their lives and communities, see Enns and Myers, *Healing Haunted Histories*.

161. For a Christian communitarian democratic socialist account of how groups on a local and household level, who are transforming the spheres of social reproduction and common life through sharing the tasks of housekeeping, child-rearing, and food procurement and preparation, fit into larger social and political transformation, see Ruether, *New Woman/New Earth*, 205–11.

162. Hossfeld and Zenger, *Psalms 3*, 478.

163. Krause, *Psalms 60–150*, 485–86.

164. Cassiodorus, *Expositio psalmarum* 132.1/*Explanation*, 3:133.

165. Bonhoeffer, *Life Together*, 27, 30–37.

166. Hossfeld and Zenger, *Psalms 3*, 479.

167. Jerome, *Homily* 45/*Homilies*, 355. Jerome, with his Scripture-shaped imagination, is tying this line together with Psalm 45:7.

168. Hossfeld and Zenger, *Psalms 3*, 480. Gutierrez, *We Drink from Our Own Wells*, 131–32. The power of common life is often similarly compartmentalized in Christian tradition as the ideals of sharing and simplicity that characterize the early Christian community described in Acts are limited to monastic community. Both Cassiodorus and Jerome, for example, make this move in their treatment of Psalm 133. Cassiodorus, *Expositio psalmarum* 132.1; Jerome, Homily 45.

169. Isasi-Diaz, "*Identifacate con Nostras*," 41–46. While the space of the "kin-dom" is certainly not limited to Latinx households, the theological wisdom and practical experience of oppressed and marginalized peoples can serve as a source of insight and correction as white and professional-class families seek to dismantle and transform structures of exploitation and oppression that mark both their public and personal lives. For additional resonant but distinct examples, see Mercy Amba Oduyoye's account of the household of God and African women's practices of care and hospitality as the basis of common life, solidarity, and alternative economies, *Introducing African Women's Theology*, chs. 6 and 7. See also Soeng Lee Kim's presentation of Korean women's exercises of political and ecological power through acts of care in *salim* hermeneutics, *Mark, Women, and Empire*, 31–37.

170. Calvin, *Commentary*, 5:165–66. Brown, *Seeing the Psalms*, 131. On approaching contemporary peacebuilding from a relational and grassroots perspective see Lederach, *Moral Imagination*, esp. ch. 8.

171. Hossfeld and Zenger, *Psalms 3*, 482–83.

172. For a mainstream account of social infrastructure, see Eric Klinenberg, *Palaces for the People*. On how these social spaces hold revolutionary potential, for example, see Zibechi's analysis of the role of plazas in the Bolivian social struggles of the early 2000s. *Dispersing Power*, 56–59.

173. For some examples on how contemporary churches in the US could be transformed through collaboration with food movements, see Woofenden, *This is God's Table*; Parish, *Resurrection Matters*; Vanderslice, *We Will Feast*; Nabhan, *Jesus for Farmers*; Dickinson, *Green Good News*. For transformation that can come through collaborating with traditions of radical democracy, see Salvatierra and Heltzel, *Faith-Rooted Organizing*; Conder and Rhodes, *Organizing Church*; Lee, *God and Community Organizing*.

174. For brief accounts of the role of the Psalms in these communities, see Randall, *Christians in the Nicaraguan Revolution*, 66–70; Simmons, *Cities of Ladies*, 78, 85.

Appendix 1—Reading the Psalms Prayerfully

ENGAGING WITH SCRIPTURE CAN be difficult. On its own, it is complex enough. The Bible is not just a book but an entire library with a vast array of texts written, edited, and collected by communities that are separated by centuries. It contains numerous genres, some of which do not have a strong analogue in our context. On top of that, we approach the Bible with all kinds of assumptions about what it is really claiming.

Reading Scripture often feels like listening in on a conversation in a language that we barely know that is dubbed over by misleading dialogue. Wait, did he actually say "blessed are the poor"? Because the dubbing made it sound like he was saying "blessed are the successful who help themselves." Can you play that back? Because it sounded like she was reciting some poem about a new political and economic order, but the voice-over was just talking about sex and the afterlife.

The best way to begin to make sense of Scripture that I know of is to read it in community. Reading this inherited wisdom in a group means pooling our knowledge and experiences so that we can begin to tease out some of the complexities and to wrestle with the implications. Yet, the insights of a single group will often get stuck in ruts. In moments of confusion or anxiety, old and unhelpful narratives will often speak up and drown out life-giving possibilities. Therefore, some of the most helpful learning communities that we have access to are not necessarily present in the flesh. Rather, this communal learning can also be engaged through reading books—learning from the insights of scholars and the wisdom of sages, saints, and prophets.

There is much to be learned from biblical scholars and theologians (and I have made suggestions for places to start at the end of this appendix and have pointed toward other paths to follow in the endnotes). Yet, the kind of understanding that is most helpful here is one that comes from practical and personal application. Engaging with the wisdom of Scripture is less like learning a body of knowledge, like mathematics, that has a relatively clear order of content to learn and answers to discover. It is more like learning a craft, where you learn from the doing, especially in collaboration with others.

This is particularly true of the prayerful poetry of the Psalter. The poetic use of language calls on us to creatively engage with our imagination, and the dynamics of communal and personal prayer demands that we, likewise, take part in these registers of language. If you read the Psalms after having only read scholars, it would be like trying to play soccer if you had only gone through practice drills but had never played the game. You might have great skill and dexterity with specific moves, but the improvisational ability and flow that come from play with others would be lost. It would be like being able to expertly produce all of the ingredients for a recipe but having no idea how to mix them together and bake. Therefore, in this appendix I want to explore *one* practice—*lectio divina*—that can help you slow down and engage the Psalms more prayerfully, playfully, and patiently.

Lectio Divina (a Latin phrase meaning "sacred reading") is a practice of reading with deep roots in Christian monasticism. It is a way to chew on words, to taste their flavor, and to make them digestible so that they may become part of us. The practice gives us a few steps to engage with a short specific passage of Scripture.

In this practice of reading, we begin by stilling ourselves and creating a spirit of receptivity. On our first reading of the selected passage, we read slowly and *listen* for a particular word, phrase, or image that strikes, or more accurately, that *caresses* us. The purpose of the first reading is not to grasp, understand, and control the whole passage, but to be open to see what aspect of the passage might reach out and take us by the hand.

Having found this connection, we sit with the image for a moment and *meditate*. This meditation leads us into reading the text a second time, now entering into it. One way of engaging with the text on this reading might be to picture ourselves within the action of the story—using our senses to see, hear, smell, touch, and taste what is around us. We might enter into the drama of Scripture by turning our chosen phrase over in our minds and teasing out the connections it has to our present situation. We can look for what kind of light this phrase or image sheds on our present surroundings and circumstances.

From this place of dwelling in the Scripture or having the Scripture dwell in our lives, we read the passage a third time in a spirit of *prayer*. We talk to God in thanksgiving, confession, and petition, while also listening for where we might be called to action and collaboration.

Finally, we sit with the text and in this prayerfully crafted abode, built by the words of Scripture and the stuff of our lives, and we rest and receive in a spirit of *contemplation*.

Reading in this way can help us cut out some of the noise so that we can listen more deeply. This includes the noise of dubbing and voice-over that our received understandings of Scripture impose, and the noise of the anxiety and busyness of our lives. We listen to Scripture in this way not to get the correct meaning, but to find the fruitful and corrective ways that Scripture can speak into our lives. We in turn bring our everyday lives to Scripture to illuminate its wisdom and promise.

The imaginative and constructive move of bringing our everyday and embodied contexts into conversation with the Scripture might be difficult for different readers for different reasons. For those who belong to oppressed communities, they may have experiences of feeling that Scripture is closed off to or even set up against them. But as Mona West proposes, one of the central moves of a feminist approach to Scripture has been to imagine who the tradition has left out or to find the radical voice in Scripture that has been obscured by unjust structures of power. Imaginatively reading Scripture alongside one's embodied and communal context could be a way of queering *lectio divina*. Reading one's life experience back into the passage can have a liberatory effect, in one's own prayerful reading and especially when shared in community.[1]

For professional-class readers, this imaginative move might be difficult because we have been taught to read dispassionately for information. For white readers it might be difficult to read these texts in terms of our context in ways that exceed our perspective as individuals, because the cultures and structures that shape our lives are often normative and dominant but they are not acknowledged as such. We can have a difficult time in understanding how the structures of culture and power are at work in our lives because we have been trained not to see them but simply to accept them. These two dynamics can make a contextual and imaginative reading of the Psalms a bit more difficult at first. Yet, if we focus on our relationships with children as parents, we can begin to find openings where we might be a little more willing to engage emotionally, explore imaginatively, and to interrogate critically the world that surrounds them and us.

There are tendencies in the monastic engagement with the Psalms to see prayerful reading as a way for reason to acquire mastery over the passions and body. I would caution against this and would instead highlight the spirit that Kathleen Norris captures when she speaks of *lectio divnia* as "a type of free-form, serious play."[2] The poetic and prayerful openings that the Psalms offer do not give us answers or knowledge that is complete or that we can possess. What they provide is a kind of energy and insight that leads us into further relationships, practices, and processes where we make a way by walking.

The interaction between life and text that this practice facilitates can serve to bring the ancient prayerful poetry of the Psalter to life. While at the same time, it can also help us see the way that God is present in our everyday lives, and it can give us different categories, norms, and values to make sense of our ordinary surroundings. If these practices are engaged communally and deepened by prophetic, critical, and childlike wisdom, we can begin to gain a different understanding and relationship with the everyday world that tacitly and unconsciously imposes the values and forms of the dominant culture on our lives and hearts. The meditations of this book are meant to show you a path to making these connections.

To assist you in engaging in this practice, below I have provided an example of a guided *lectio divina* that you can use in solitude, an account of how this practice of reading might be used in community, and some direction for further study.

A Guided Lectio Divina for Use in Solitude

Still yourself, find a comfortable posture, close your eyes, picture a calm place in your mind, and go there. Let the stillness and silence wash over you like a warm shower, and breathe. Settle into that space for about a minute and open yourself up to God.

[1 minute]

Open your eyes and read over the passage you have chosen. Read it slowly and gently. Do not grope yet for an overall meaning but listen to the words. Keep your eyes open for a word or phrase that catches you. Is there one that appears to be typed in bold? Is there a phrase that jumps out and grabs you by the hand? As you read, do so watchfully and attentively listening for this kind of connection.

[3–4 minutes]

Return to this word or phrase and repeat it in your head, not willfully but as a mantra or a song. Let its associations and connections to your life and thoughts unfold. You might imagine yourself in the place of the drama or setting of the text, or you might hear its words as relevant to something going on in your life right now. What are you hearing in these ancient symbols today?

[3–4 minutes]

Once again, go back to the passage and read it again. This time take the entire passage in and ponder its meaning in relationship to the word or words you have been contemplating. What does this landscape look like with this object placed at the forefront? What does the picture look like after having bathed this little word in light? How does this speak to your heart in the stillness of this moment?

[3–4 minutes]

Having entered into this conversation with this passage, listening for its words, turning them over, and connecting them to your own thoughts, emotions, and life, you might want to speak with God. Use words, images, or ideas. Speak freely in your mind as though you were conversing with a close friend. Share with God what you have found in your heart.

[3–4 minutes]

Rest in this space. Allow your body, mind, and spirit to settle into the stillness of this room. Follow your breath, allowing it to rise and fall. And open your ears and heart to this moment and to the other gifts this day will present you.

[3–4 minutes]

An Outline of Lectio Divina for Communal Use

The Green Christians Dinner Church that my wife and I host is largely organized around this practice of prayerful reading. When we gather together, we have an extended period of slowing down and connecting as we eat a simple meal and share our joys and concerns. My wife, who is a clinical social worker, has taught me a helpful way of viewing the order of operation for a significant conversation: regulate, relate, and then rationalize. Viewed through this lens the meal, then, serves as a way for us to nourish and care for our bodies. The prayerful sharing of what is going on in our lives puts us in a relational posture of mutual care. This work allows us to then read in a way that is open, collaborative, critical, and creative. This kind of preparatory work could be pursued in any number of other ways, but it is helpful to spend some time to shape the space.

When we read Scripture together, we do so by reading the text three times. The first time we read it listening for a phrase that grabs our attention. We then have an open conversation where we begin to wrestle with the text from the perspective of this image. In this first part of our conversation, we try to focus on discerning what is happening in the text. Our comments are often driven by a sense of curiosity or wonder about what a certain part means within its historical context or in a wider theological scope. On the second reading we listen for how the passage connects to our lives. Invariably we have already been making these connections, but during this period we place greater emphasis on considering how the dynamics at work in the passage might have a direct analogy to something that is going on in our world. For our last reading we listen for where we are being called to act in the coming weeks. We conclude our time together by celebrating communion.

This loose structure provides a container that holds us together. No one is burdened with the task of being an expert (though it does help to have a facilitator to gently return the conversation to the process). In this practice, we are given a cooperative space to find connection, correction, and inspiration.

Starting Places for Further Study

Lectio Divina and Contextual Reading

Vest, *No Moment Too Small*, ch 2. West, "Queer *Lectio Divina*." Isaisi-Diaz, *Mujerista Theology*, chs. 1 and 2.

Appendix 1—Reading the Psalms Prayerfully

Parenting and Spirituality

Miller McLemore, *In the Midst of Chaos*. Wylie-Kellerman, ed., *Sandbox Revolution*.

Liberating Spirituality

Carvalhaes, *Praying with Every Heart*. Townes, *In a Blaze of Glory*. McLaren, *Finding Our Way Again*.

Praying the Psalms

Davis, *Getting Involved with God*, part 1. Brueggemann, *Praying the Psalms*.

Introducing the Psalms

Stuessey, *Psalms*. Brown, *Psalms*.

Going Deeper with the Psalms

Walker-Jones, *Green Psalter*. Brown, *Seeing the Psalms*. Brueggemann, *Psalms and the Life of Faith*.

Commentaries on the Psalms

Schaefer, *Psalms*. Gillingham, *Psalms through the Centuries*. Brueggemann and Bellinger, *Psalms*.

Devotional Life with the Psalms

Cudjoe-Wilkes and Wilkes, *Psalms for Black Lives*. Chittister, *The Psalms*. Bourgeault, *Chanting the Psalms*.

Reading Scriptures through a Green Lens

Davis, *Scripture, Culture, and Agriculture*. Dickinson, *Green Good News*.

Appendix 2—Spiritual Exercises for Personal and Communal Engagement

In this appendix you will find suggestions for engaging the Psalms and themes of each meditation. For each chapter I have provided two sets of questions, one concerned with spiritual practice and another focused on everyday life. I have also provided a suggested spiritual exercise. These are offered up to be used personally or with a group.

If you are engaging the questions on your own, I would invite you to journal. The act of writing is often a practice of discovery. While we can certainly be surprised by our own train of thought, I find that the exercise of putting words to a page is often more effective in teasing out distinctions that were tangled in my mind, in surfacing truths that were stuffed under, and in hearing the surprising song of the Spirit that comes from beyond us.

Whether these questions are used as the basis of reflection or group discussion, please do not feel obliged to answer them all, and certainly not all at once. The primary question is placed in italics. It is followed by leading questions that might help you gain some momentum or add some flesh to the question. Please do not let the additional questions overwhelm you. This is not a test. You will not be graded as to how well you address all of the questions. When I was first making the shift from graduate student to teaching undergraduates I would often pile question upon question on the conversation. This was in part due to my zeal for the materials and course, and partly out of an anxiety and reluctance to really let the question breathe and to let the discussion get out of my hands. Rather than cultivating conversation, it suffocated it. So with these questions, whether you are journaling on your own or reflecting in a group, find the question that grabs you and give it a chance to stretch its legs and your imagination.

As you read over these questions and exercises you may, at times, wonder: what does this have to do with climate change? The exercises provided here are likely a bit different from the "green" or "nature" oriented material that you likely have encountered before. The focus of the materials in this appendix is to attend to the norms and structures that are blocking our collective paths to justice and joy, *and* to cultivating the practices of love that can empower us to begin to nurture the communities that are capable of cooperating for a new world.

Chapter 1

Reflection on Spiritual Practice

Who or what do you most fundamentally trust for security, sustenance, and joy? In what parts of your life do you demonstrate this trust? How would you describe the shepherd you are following? How might someone else answer if they only saw your life from the outside and did not know what your internal life was like? What practices have built this trust? How might trust be built spiritually? Who or what do you think your children are being taught to trust?

Reflection on Everyday Life

What does the word "comfort" mean to you? Where do you find comfort? What makes you comfortable? What does comfort mean in relation to distress? What does comfort mean in relationship to lifestyle? What is required for you to be comfortable? What is your general response to discomfort? How does that affect your ability to be with or support others? Are there competing understandings of comfort in your life? What is a vision of comfort that would be healing for you and inviting for others? What understanding of comfort do you want your children to have? What vision of comfort will be most helpful to the next generation living in a changed climate?

Spiritual Exercise

Picturing Justice and Joy. Where does the *good* shepherd lead you? Psalm 23 offers us the two images of green pastures and welcoming banquets. In group or in solitude, read the psalm and then engage your imagination to think about what a space of justice and joy would look like. If you are engaging with children, drawing a picture would likely be the most appropriate approach. If you are with a group of adults, perhaps some will want to draw and others would prefer to give a narrative account. Spend some time thinking about what the place looks and feels like. What is at the center of this picture? What kind of relationships does it foster between neighbor, land, and God?

Chapter 2

Reflection on Spiritual Practice

Where are you able to make a joyful noise to the Lord? Do you regularly sing in the choir or only when you are alone in the car? What role did music play in your life as a child or an adolescent? What role does music play in the life of your children or the children around you? In what ways do you see this as a spiritual practice, an act of worship, a kind of prayer? What are the aspects of making a joyful noise that would qualify it as praise or prayer? How could you make space for more of this in your life and community? If you do not consider yourself to be musical or to have musical talent, what are some ways that you can *participate* in making a joyful noise? What are some creative ways you might join the chorus of creation?

Reflection on Everyday Life

What are the environments like where you work, live, and play? Are they similar to each other or is it as though they exist in separate worlds? What kinds of communities and lives do these environments shape? Are there types of jobs, roles, and relationships that have ready-made niches and others that do not fit? What does that mean for children growing up in this place? What are the relationships between these environments and those of people of different classes and races? If you were to describe one of these environments in the terms we use for natural habitats and yourself as a creature in those, what would they be? Is work like a jungle with predators, a desert with scavengers, a prairie with a herd, etc.?

Spiritual Exercise

Follow the lead of a critter. Take some time to pay attention to a creature, preferably one whose perspective is a bit more in proximity to the ground. This might mean following an ant from the driveway into the grass, following the path of a squirrel in the park, or following a child in the backyard. Before you start on this expedition with your fellow creature you might want to take some time to still and center yourself. While you are following, see how tactilely engaged you can become. Attempt to engage all of your senses in what the critter is doing.

Afterwards, take inventory of what you saw. How did this change what you now see about this place? How does this creature's life intersect with your own? How do you feel after giving your attention to this critter and its path? Draw out the implications of this feeling. For example, if you feel a sense of calm, you might consider how this is different from paths that make you feel differently. If you feel silly, you might consider what paths you consider serious and why they seem more significant.

Chapter 3

Reflection on Spiritual Practice

When you were a child and you were taught to pray, was there a place to share struggles and name larger problems? Was there a place for lament? What kinds of expectations were you given for how God would respond? Did God have a plan that would ultimately manage the issues or did this plan render these laments insignificant? Was God beside you in your grief? Did you feel shame about offering a complaint? In your childhood was there a discomfort with the language of prayer in general? Was it seen as superstitious, irrelevant, or perhaps too vulnerable? Who did you hear prayerfully give voice to injuries and injustice? How have these childhood experiences shaped your prayer life today? How have you or might you share this with your children?

Reflection on Everyday Life

What is your typical response when you are in a situation where you are not in control? What if the situation is not chaos, but it is collaborative, like a group project or a church workday? Do you try to take the reins? Do you go with the flow? Are you easily frustrated? Do you check out? Do you interact with curiosity and patience? What if the situation involves your children, and nothing is imminently dangerous, but they are running a bit wild? What if the situation is simply talking about something that is systemic and unjust? What if the situation is a personal or family crisis? Are there external factors that make it easier or more difficult to dwell in situations with others that cannot be easily managed?

Spiritual Exercise

Communal Lament. While cultural norms might often push us to manage or solve problems, often what people facing loss, fear, despair, and hopelessness need is simply someone there to hold them (proverbially or literally). This capacity to dwell in the darkness with others is a capability that we can exercise. The lament Psalms give us words and structures to do so.

With a group, or perhaps with your children or one of your children, gather together to pray Psalm 13. You will need the psalm, strips of paper and writing utensils, a candle, and a place where the paper can burn.

Leader: Let us still ourselves in preparation to open our hearts to God and one another.

All: Read Psalm 13:1–2.

Leader: Take a few moments to write about what is weighing on your hearts. These struggles could be personal, but I especially invite you to offer up laments about the bigger troubles that we all face.

All: Read Psalm 13:3–4.

Leader: Now we will commit our prayers to the flame, as a sign that we are offering them to God. While we know that this will not take the anxiety or fear away, we pray that the burden may be made a bit lighter as we are no longer left to carry them by ourselves.

[Burning of laments.]

All: Read Psalm 13:4–6.

Leader: Let us still ourselves in this moment, acknowledging the fear and pain that remains, dwelling in this difficult place together, and turning to God in hope.

[Leader, gently check in on people after the litany. The purpose is not to solve but to be present. If anyone appears shaken, especially if it is one of your children, check in on them again in an hour or two.]

Chapter 4

Reflection on Spiritual Practice

Are there everyday tasks that feel prayerful to you? Are there routines that help you feel centered or at peace? Are there acts of care that seem to deepen or renew connections? What kinds of small actions do you find reorienting or that call you beyond yourself? Are there chores or responsibilities you have where you enter "the zone" or where you lose yourself in a kind of joyful simple action? What sorts of activities do the children in your life engage in that seem to have these qualities? What is it about these activities that make them different? Is it about how other people relate to them or value your contribution? Where they fit in the rhythm of your day? Who you do them with or for? How you were taught or initiated into doing them?

Reflection on Everyday Life

How are labors of care valued in your context and community? Where would they fit on a continuum of being taken for granted or valorized? Are they equitably distributed or are they largely heaped on one person? How do they fit into the daily rhythm? Are they central or are they squeezed in when there is time? What is the relationship between your workplace and these acts of care (support, antagonism, competition, etc.)? Are these acts carried out by the household or are part of these performed by paid laborers? If the latter, what are the class, race, and gender dynamics between your household and these caregivers? Is there much agency in these kinds of decisions, or do external time, economic, and social pressures largely constrain these rhythms and relationships? What role do your children or do other people's children play in these activities?

Appendix 2—Spiritual Exercises for Personal and Communal Engagement

Spiritual Exercise

Examining moments of care. This exercise is a modified version of a form of prayer most commonly associated with the Jesuit practice of examen. In this prayer, you will review your day looking for where God was at work. I encourage you to pursue this prayer with a sense of gentleness and curiosity, rather than one of harsh judgement or shame.

Take a few moments to still yourself, find your breath, and open your heart to the spirit of God.

Review your day, moving backwards. You might orient yourself by looking back at each hour one at a time, or you might look at different segments of your day in relation to meals or with your change in location. As you review each period of your day, turn a spotlight on acts of care. Moments when you received or gave care in the form of food, a kind gesture, a supportive conversation, a moment of levity, an item or activity that nurtured your body or spirit.

As you attend to these moments, having your mind's eye zoom up close, think about who was providing care and how they did so. You might think about the nature of your relationship, and what it is like on each side to be a part of this interaction. You might think about how these acts of care fit into the rhythm of your day. That is, was the interaction as short as possible for convenience's sake, lingered over, routinized and overlooked? You might consider the affect that accompanied that moment and what you are feeling now as you look back on it. You might ponder the role that the wider space and place played in the character of this act. You might think about how this act of care connects to other similar acts, and what that means.

As you examine these moments, linger a bit to see where the light and love of God are at work or are perhaps overlooked. If these moments arise again, how might you acknowledge or channel this love and light? How could you have attended to these moments of care differently? Try not to ask this question with the cringes of regret or neurotic self-blame. Look for the openings of these moments, as much as you can, as promises and promptings of hope.

End this time of prayer with a word of thanksgiving for the creatures and the wider creation that make your small and precious life possible.

Chapter 5

Reflection on Spiritual Practice

What sorts of stories captured your imagination as a child and how did this shape your life of faith? Think both of Bible stories and other stories and genres from the wider culture. How did these shape your understanding of God? Is God a binding and transcendent force? An overbearing father figure? A judge or referee ready to dole out trophies and punishments? A serene spirit that is ever present but often overlooked? A magical figure with a big plan? How did these figures shape your understanding of what a life of faith was supposed to look like? Is the person of faith a hero, a gifted person that does a remarkable thing? A hardworking underdog who plays by the rules and wins in the end? An individual who will go their own way regardless of the obstacles? An unlikely champion of the people from humble beginnings? A group of people deeply committed to one another and driven by a shared dream? A tragic figure who must give everything for the greater good?

Reflection on Everyday Life

What sort of stories get told in your community (in movies, television, sermons, articles, features, gossip, family discussions)? Who are the sorts of people stories are told about? Who are the heroes? What are the heroic actions? Who are the villains? What are the animating conflicts? What does happily ever after look like? Are you and your children presented with similar types of stories? (If this feels too open-ended, perhaps, take a look at the home page of your favorite news outlet, or track social media for a day, or look at your viewing history for a streaming service, or look back over the sermons of the last two months.)

Spiritual Exercise

Collaborative Storytelling—If you have a young child in your life, write a story with them. My son and I do this collaboratively as we come up with a title or theme together, and then one of us will assume a character. Typically he is "Ed" and I am "Pip." We take turns contributing the dialogue for each of our characters and let a story unfold. The stories tend to be winding, to stall out, and sometimes derivative of something else we are currently reading. But we find it to be fun to dance in our imaginations together to write a story, to exercise our capacity to tell and not simply to receive stories, and to sometimes indirectly explore a topic he is thinking about.

If this option is not available to you, perhaps you could try your hand at telling a children's story. Nothing complex. Perhaps a brief parable.

Chapter 6

Reflection on Spiritual Practice

What role does envy, anxiety, anger, and fear play in your prayer life and in your broader life of faith? Is prayer cathartic, a place of peace, a source of these emotions, or a bit of each? Is prayer a space to speak freely or a tightly scripted performance? Are people in your faith community able to express these emotions and if so in what ways or about what? What sorts of external forces or contexts stoke these emotions for you? Where do you feel them in your body? What sort of response do they evoke? Fight? Flight? Freeze? Appease? What role do these emotions play in the communities you are a part of? Where are they expressed or repressed? What sort of responses do they evoke from the social body? How does this shape your approach to being a parent? Or how is this shaped by the realities of parenting?

Reflection on Everyday Life

Where do you look for happiness, success, and security? Would the way you answer this question if you were telling your children be different from the implied script that you might live out? What implicit visions of happiness, success, and security could be drawn out by looking at where you put your money, your ambitions for work or the future, and your politics? To what degree are these matters about your personal preferences, or are they about the social worlds and economic and political structures that shape your life? Are there different or even contradictory scripts that are at work in different parts of your life? Are there openings, however small, for you to practice living out a different vision?

Spiritual Exercise

Imagining the script. There are many forms of prayer that invite readers to imagine themselves into the scene in a passage of Scripture. One might assume the position of a main character, a bystander, or someone who is often marginalized in our reading of the story. By attending to each of our senses, one by one, we can begin to incarnate the story in our imaginations. The poetry of the Psalter makes this kind of engagement a bit more difficult. But for this exercise, find a script that is at work in the psalm. Attend to a line or follow a thread in the poem and try to imagine what life would look like in light of this poetry. Find an entry point around an action, an image, or a figure and try and put your feet down. (Bonus points if this person is a parent or child in the scene.) Look at the setting around you. Look for the social context and the tensions it names. Gaze ahead and discern the ideal that this image is striving toward or the injustice that it is weighed down by. Attend to this space and dwell in it prayerfully. As you do so imagine the social script that is at work. What does it feel like? How does it connect to the spaces and scripts you find in your shared life?

Chapter 7

Reflection on Spiritual Practice

In what ways does prayer or your life of faith lead you upward and outward, or in what ways does it leave you stuck looking inward? What do you feel guilty about? How do you process feelings of guilt? To what degree are you responsible, complicit, or simply compelled to be a part of that which inspires your guilt? Are there patterns of disavowal where these feelings are stuffed under and thereby become increasingly haunting? Do these feelings help you to be more compassionate toward others or to strive to be centered on higher hopes? Are there spaces or times when guilt is named in a communal or shared way in your communities? In what ways is your spiritual journey a private matter, or in what ways does it turn you to reach out to others and to work for transformation? Would you describe the spiritual journey of your children in a similar way?

Reflection on Everyday Life

In what ways do your practices of parenting and life at home lead you upward and outward, or in what ways do they direct you inward? In what ways does your care for your children and the way your home is structured turn your family inwards away from the wider world, or does it empower you all for the work of justice? Are there structures or social realities that determine this for your family (like the demands of work, the specifics of geography and neighborhood, etc.)? What positive role might a more inward-looking refuge play in more social and communal efforts? Are there seasons of our life where we should be turned inward? Is caring for children an inherently social and outward-looking act? Are there specific ways that we can foster a shared life in a family that will nurture justice in future communities?

Spiritual Exercise

Communal Confession—Write a corporate prayer of confession. If possible, do so in collaboration with others. Start by taking some time to write down a few of the ways that your life is entangled with unsustainable systems (food, transportation, real estate, etc.), the ways that you willingly serve these systems, and the ways that you feel coerced or stuck in relying on them. Then take a moment to review these and to consider the specific relationships that these systems and realities have damaged (relationships with other persons, communities, creatures, and habitats). Then try to find some language to name what the practices and forms of an alternative life might look like (this could be by naming specific models that you might be aware of or simply finding words like reparation, restoration, and justice that help you begin to reach toward imagining what healing would look like).

With these materials in hand, pray Psalm 130 (or adapt this liturgy to pray in solitude).

All: Out of the depths I cry to you, O Lord. Lord, hear my voice! Let your ears be attentive to the voice of my supplications! If you, O Lord, should mark iniquities, Lord, who could stand?

Leader: God we confess the ways that our lives are caught up in and complicit with systems that injure your creatures and your creation.

All: [An offering of confessions as participants are comfortable.]

Leader: But there is forgiveness with you, so that you may be revered.

All: I wait for the Lord; my soul waits, and in his word I hope; my soul waits for the Lord more than those who watch for the morning.

Leader: We wait in expectant hope for your forgiveness and new life. We set our hearts on these hopes.

All: [An offering of names or images of what healing or new life might look like.]

Leader: O Israel, hope in the Lord!

All: For with the Lord there is steadfast love, and with him is great power to redeem. It is he who will redeem Israel from all its iniquities. AMEN.

Chapter 8

Reflection on Spiritual Practice

How does your community cultivate a spirit of celebration? What sorts of activities are used to express praise, thanksgiving, and joy? What role does God or the language of faith traditions play? What is explicitly celebrated? What might be unnamed but assumed and at the heart of the celebration? Where does this celebration take place? How is this resonant or dissonant with your experiences of communal celebration as a child? What role are children given in celebration? What role do you play?

Reflection on Everyday Life

During what festive time of the year do you and your family and/or community currently find a deep sense of connection and joy? Is this a holiday, an explicitly religious observance, a vacation, a music festival, a camping trip? What is it about the rhythms of these days that are different from other days? What is it that you are all gathered around? What facilitates or fosters your connection and time together? What does this time look, smell, sound, taste, and feel like? How could this time be reorienting, so that you approach other parts of your shared lives differently? Are there ways that this time could be expanded into other parts of the year?

Spiritual Exercise

The songs of our lives. The things we learn by heart shape our hearts. Music especially has this power. It also often has the power to connect us to others as we sing together.

Think of a song or a genre of music that you associate with joy, deep connection, and perhaps festive celebration. Take some time and listen to this music prayerfully—which may mean in stillness or as you dance. Allow the music to transport you to past memories or to carry you forward to future hopes. Follow your muscle memory and allow the words and melodies to flow through you.

After spending some time in celebration, take some time to reflect on what it is about the music that brought you joy. What associations? What sensibilities, lyrics, or moods internal to the music? Does it still do so? How might music help you make more room for shared joy and praise in your everyday life? Is there a way that this could serve as an opening to a different kind of community, to different rhythms?

Chapter 9

Reflection on Spiritual Practice

Where can you find yourself caught up in play? Does it depend on the time, the game, the players, the place? What were your favorite games or activities to play as a child? Who were you closest playmates? What places or groups of people were easiest to play with? What is the place of play in your life now? What kinds of play do the children in your life engage in? How might you make more room for play in your life now? What would it take for you to see play as sacred or revolutionary?

Reflection on Everyday Life

What kind of work ethic do you have? Where do you think you learned or inherited it? What does it value? What kind of emotional range is appropriate in your work ethic? How does your desired work ethic match up with what is expected from people at your workplace? How does it shape your daily rhythms? How does it shape your time and relationships at home? How does it shape your time and relationships with friends, a faith community, or the broader community? Would you say that you work to live or that you live to work? What kind of work ethic do you hope to pass on to the children in your life?

Spiritual Exercise

Dreaming of the day when. The philosopher Ernst Bloch proposed that there was a potential for great change in the practice of daydreaming. Whereas our dreams at night are often detached from reality and about processing repressed fears from our past, daydreams are an altered version of reality. They are about a life that is real enough to picture, but with some aspects changed for a more beautiful, shared life. Daydreaming is a practice of hope that imagines a better future.[3]

Spend some time daydreaming. Find a comfortable place to sit and a good window to look out. Let your eyes wonder and wander, let them gaze without focus, and go inward. But as you go inward, go outward in picturing a life of justice and joy. What does that look like on your little patch of creation? Try to do this without a timer, or without the tyranny of the practical breathing down your neck. Take some stolen moments to develop your capacity to hope and dream.

Chapter 10

Reflection on Spiritual Practice

Where is the rich soil in your life where you can sow seeds of change that will be nurtured and grow over time? What spiritual gifts do you have? What are the spiritual gifts of the children in your life? What are the life-giving relationships that are or that have been in your life? What are the spaces or communities where you find joy, or clarity, or connection, or courage, or healing? Who are the people who might be your allies or co-conspirators in the long work of growing transformative community? What role do the children in your life play in these spaces and relationships? What communities would you like to see nurture them? How might they be invited into or lead this work?

Reflection on Everyday Life

How can you introduce a transformative social practice into the rhythms of your life? When might there be time in your schedule for this? How could you make time? What already scheduled meeting, group, or routine might be repurposed so that you have time? How can this practice be organized to fit within the lives of others (especially the children in your life) so that it is shared and there is mutual accountability and encouragement? Is there a time of the week when the rhythms of other activities will make it easier for you to more fully engage this practice? What obstacles do you foresee in making time? Other commitments? Scripts about work, responsibility, productivity, and what is truly valuable? Systemic pressures of supervisors, debt, caregiving, and peers? What can you do to be patient enough with the practice to allow it to grow, to allow something that is initially small to be enough and to be protected from external demands?

Spiritual Exercise

Starting with the margins. The word *margin* is meant in a dual sense—first referring to the extra that exceeds need and second designating the spaces and peoples who are excluded and exploited by unjust systems.

First, finding a margin. Though we are often told that we are sovereign deciders that exercise complete freedom in our lives, we live in a world of limits. The demands on time, energy, and resources are real. If we try to step out as heroic individuals to take on massive systems, our efforts will likely be crushed under the weight of the commitments and compulsions that these systems place on us. Yet, if we are creative, courageous, and careful we can likely find some margin in our lives—a little extra bit of time and energy that is not claimed by need. At the heart of discovering this margin is entering a process where we can begin to differentiate between assumed and actual need.

To find this margin, engage in the practice of examen for a week (described in the spiritual exercise for chapter 4). Only this time, as you prayerfully look back on your day, make note of times and spaces where there is some extra room. This is not about cutting out waste so that you can maximize the productivity of each moment. Rather, it is about finding those openings where a shared time might be repurposed, or about discerning what routine or activity is more of a fetter than a necessity, which could be released to create time and energy for something else. Make note of the openings, and at the end of the week look for a pattern where you might plant the seeds of change.

Second, learning from the margins. If we want to understand and transform unjust systems the margins are typically the places with the clearest vision. From these spaces we can understand how these systems truly work, and we can break through the internal and internalized narratives and scripts that often mask these cruel realities. Furthermore, the communities that have been forced to live on the margins have often gained intergenerational wisdom about what resistance and resilience looks like in life-long struggle. Finally, the grassroots power that is needed to transform systems will be derived, in part, from these communities. Yet, white and professional-class people will often enter into these spaces not seeking to learn but to lead, not looking to stand in solidarity but to act as saviors. For this reason, we should look for existing peoples and justice movements and community projects and coalitions where there is an invitation to enter into this work in a way that fosters humility, mutuality, and equity.[4]

To discern where these openings might be, enter into a season of listening. Pay attention to what your friends, kids, and other parents are doing. Look for announcements and invitations in your community, schools, churches, or in broader networks. Start showing up in a spirit of curiosity and patience. In this season the task is not to find a solution, but to discern where there are relationships and movements where you can begin to connect and collaborate.

Endnotes

Appendix 1

1. West, "Queer *Lectio Divina*," 372–73, 377–78.
2. Norris, *Amazing Grace*, 277–78.

Appendix 2

3. See Weeks, *Problem with Work*, 190–98.
4. For some guidance on thinking through these dynamics I recommend Shannon Craigo-Snell and Christopher Doucot, *No Innocent Bystanders*.

Bibliography

Ahmed, Sara. *The Promise of Happiness*. Durham, NC: Duke University Press, 2010.

Alston, Dana, ed. *We Speak for Ourselves: Social Justice, Race, and Environment*. Washington, DC: Panos Institute, 1990.

Alter, Robert. *The Book of Psalms: A Translation with Commentary*. New York: W. W. Norton, 2007.

Alves, Rubem. *Tomorrow's Child: Imagination, Creativity, and the Rebirth of Culture*. New York: Harper & Row, 1972.

Ambrose. *Commentary of Saint Ambrose on Twelve Psalms*. Translated by Ide Ni Riain. Dublin: Halcyon, 2000.

————. "Of Naboth." In *Ambrose*, Edited and Translated by Boniface Ramsey, 117–44. New York: Routledge, 1997.

Athanasius. *Letter to Marcellinus on the Interpretation of the Psalms*, in *The Life of Anthony* and *Letter to Marcellinus*, translated by Robert Gregg, 101–29. New York: Paulist, 1980.

Augustine. *The City of God*. Books I–VII. Washington, DC: Catholic University of America Press, 2008.

————. *Expositions of the Psalms 1–32*. Translated by Maria Boulding. New York: New City, 2000.

————. *Expositions of the Psalms 73–98*. Translated by Maria Boulding. New York: New City, 2002.

Baker-Fletcher, Karen. *Sisters of Dust, Sisters of Spirit: Womanist Wordings on God and Creation*. Minneapolis: Fortress, 1998.

Basil. *On Social Justice*. Translated by Paul Schroeder. Crestwood, NY: St. Vladimir's Seminary Press, 2009.

Blake, William. "London." In *The Portable Blake*, 112. New York: Penguin, 1976.

Blosser, Joe. "And It Was Good: Building an Ethics of Sufficiency." *Journal of the Society of Christian Ethics* 41.1 (2021) 3–19.

Bonhoeffer, Dietrich. *Life Together* and *Prayerbook of the Bible*. Minneapolis: Fortress, 2005.

Boulton, Mathew Myer. *Life in God: John Calvin, Practical Formation, and the Future of Protestant Theology*. Grand Rapids: Eerdmans, 2011.

Bourgeault, Cynthia. *Chanting the Psalms*. Boston: New Seeds, 2006.

Braude, William, ed. *The Midrash on Psalms*. Vol. 1. New Haven: Yale University Press, 1959.

Bibliography

Brock, Rita Nakashima. *Journeys by Heart: A Christology of Erotic Power.* New York: Crossroad, 1988.

Brown, Wendy. *Undoing the Demos: Neoliberalism's Stealth Revolution.* Brooklyn: Zone, 2015.

Brown, William. *Psalms.* Nashville: Abingdon, 2010.

———. *Seeing the Psalms: A Theology of Metaphor.* Louisville: Westminster John Knox, 2002.

———. *The Seven Pillars of Creation: The Bible, Science, and the Ecology of Wonder.* New York: Oxford University Press, 2010.

Brueggemann, Walter. *Praying the Psalms: Engaging Scripture and the Life of the Spirit.* Eugene, OR: Cascade, 2007.

———. *The Psalms and the Life of Faith.* Minneapolis: Fortress, 1995.

Brueggemann, Walter, and William Bellinger. *Psalms.* New York: Cambridge University Press, 2014.

Buck-Morss, Susan. *The Dialectics of Seeing: Walter Benjamin and the Arcades Project.* Cambridge: MIT Press, 1989.

Calvin, John. *Commentary on the Book of Psalms.* 5 vols. Edited by James Anderson. Grand Rapids: Eerdmans, 1949.

———. "The Form of Prayers and Songs of the Church." *Calvin Theological Journal* 15.2 (1980) 160–65.

———. *Institutes of Christian Religion.* Edited by John McNeil. Philadelphia: Westminster, 1960.

Caputo, John D. *The Weakness of God: A Theology of the Event.* Bloomington: Indiana University Press, 2006.

Cardenal, Ernesto. *Psalms.* New York: Crossroad, 1981.

Carter, Christopher. *The Spirit of Soul Food: Race, Faith and Food Justice.* Urbana, IL: University of Illinois Press.

Carvalhaes, Claudio. *Liturgies from Below: Praying with People at the End of the World.* Nashville: Abingdon, 2020.

———. *Praying with Every Heart: Orienting Our Lives to the Wholeness of the World.* Eugene, OR: Cascade, 2021.

———. *Ritual at World's End: Essays on Eco-Liturgical Liberation Theology.* York, PA: Barber's Son, 2021.

Casey, Michael. *Athirst for God: Spiritual Desire in Bernard of Clairvaux's Sermons on the Song of Songs.* Kalamazoo, MI: Cistercian 1988.

Cassian, John. *The Conferences.* Translated by Boniface Ramsey. New York: Paulist, 1997.

Cassiodorus. *Explanation of the Psalms.* 3 vols. Translated by P. G. Walsh. New York: Paulist, 1990–1991.

Chittister, Joan. *The Psalms: Meditations for Every Day of the Year.* New York: Crossroad, 1996.

———. *Wisdom Distilled from the Daily: Living the Rule of St. Benedict Today.* New York: Harper One, 1990.

Chrysostom, John. *Commentary on the Psalms.* Vol. 2. Translated by Robert Charles Hill. Brookline, MA: Holy Cross Orthodox Press, 1998.

Clapp, Rodney. *Naming Neoliberalism: Exposing the Spirit of Our Age.* Minneapolis: Fortress, 2021.

Clifford, Richard J. *Psalms 1–72.* Nashville: Abingdon, 2002.

Bibliography

Conder, Tim, and Dan Rhodes. *Organizing Church: Grassroots Practices for Embodying Change in Your Congregation, Your Community, and Our World.* St. Louis: Chalice, 2017.

Craigo-Snell, Shannon, and Christopher Doucot. *No Innocent Bystanders: Becoming an Ally in the Struggle for Justice.* Louisville: Westminster John Knox, 2017.

Cudjoe-Wilkes, Gabby, and Andrew Wilkes. *Psalms for Black Lives: Reflections for the Work of Liberation.* Nashville: Abingdon, 2022.

Culp, Kristine. *Vulnerability and Glory: A Theological Account.* Louisville: Westminster John Knox, 2011.

Daley, Brian. "Finding the Right Key: The Aims and Strategies of Early Christian interpretation of the Psalms." In *Psalms in Community: Jewish and Christian Textual, Liturgical, and Artistic Traditions,* edited by Harold Attridge and Margot Fassler, 189–206. Boston: Brill, 2003.

Dardot, Pierre, and Christian Laval. *The New Way of the World: On Neo-Liberal Society.* New York: Verso, 2013.

Dauvergne, Peter. *Environmentalism of the Rich.* Cambridge: MIT Press, 2016.

Davis, Ellen. *Getting Involved with God: Rediscovering the Old Testament.* Chicago: Cowley, 2001.

———. *Scripture, Culture, and Agriculture: An Agrarian Reading of the Bible.* New York: Cambridge University Press, 2008.

Day, Dorothy. *Loaves and Fishes.* Maryknoll, NY: Orbis, 1997.

Day, Keri. *Religious Resistance to Neoliberalism: Womanist and Black Feminist Perspectives.* New York: Palgrave MacMillan, 2016.

Dickinson, T. Wilson. *Exercises in New Creation from Paul to Kierkegaard.* New York: Palgrave MacMillan, 2018.

———. *The Green Good News: Christ's Path to Joyful and Sustainable Life.* Eugene, OR: Cascade, 2019.

Eberhart, Timothy. *Rooted and Grounded in Love: Holy Communion for the Whole Creation.* Eugene, OR: Pickwick, 2017.

Ehrenreich, Barbara, and John Ehrenreich. *Death of a Yuppie Dream: The Rise and Fall of the Professional-Managerial Class.* New York: Rosa Luxemburg Siftung, 2013.

Enns, Elaine, and Ched Myers. *Healing Haunted Histories: A Settler Discipleship of Decolonization.* Eugene, OR: Cascade, 2021.

Federici, Silvia. *Re-Enchanting the World: Feminism and the Politics of the Commons.* Oakland, CA: PM, 2019.

Fishbane, Michael. *Sacred Attunement: A Jewish Theology.* Chicago: University of Chicago Press, 2008.

Foster, Richard. *Freedom of Simplicity.* San Francisco: Harper & Row, 1981.

Foucault, Michel. *The Birth of Biopolitics: Lectures at the Collège de France 1978–79.* New York: Palgrave Macmillan, 2008.

———. *Security, Territory, Population: Lectures at the Collège de France, 1977–78.* New York: Palgrave MacMillan, 2007.

Francis (Pope). *Laudato si'.* Vatican City: Vatican, 2015.

Fraser, Nancy. "Contradictions of Capital and Care." *New Left Review* 100 (2016) 99–117.

Fraser, Nancy, and Rahel Jaeggi. *Capitalism: A Conversation in Critical Theory.* Medford, MA: Polity, 2018.

Gafney, Wilda C. *Womanist Midrash: A Reintroduction to the Women of the Torah and the Throne.* Louisville: Westminster John Knox, 2017.

Bibliography

Gandolfo, Elizabeth O'Donnell. *The Power and Vulnerability of Love: A Theological Anthropology*. Minneapolis: Fortress, 2015.

Garcia-Rivera, Alejandro. *The Community of the Beautiful: A Theological Aesthetics*. Collegeville, MN: Liturgical, 1999.

Garrigan, Siobhan. "The Hermeneutics of Intersubjectivity: A Study of Theologies of Homelessness." In *Grace, Governance, and Globalization*, edited by Stephan van Erp et al., 62–76. London: Bloomsbury, 2017.

Gillingham, Susan. *Psalms Through the Centuries: A Reception History Commentary on Psalms 1–72*. Hoboken, NJ: Wiley Blackwell, 2018.

Goizueta, Roberto. *Caminemos Con Jesus: Toward a Hispanic/Latino Theology of Accompaniment*. Maryknoll, NY: Orbis, 1997.

———. "Fiesta: Life in the Subjunctive." In *From the Heart of Our People: Latino/a Explorations in Catholic Systematic Theology*, edited by Miguel Diaz and Orlando Espin, 84–99. Maryknoll, NY: Orbis, 1999.

Goto, Courtney. *The Grace of Playing: Pedagogies for Leaning into God's New Creation*. Eugene, OR: Pickwick, 2016.

Gregory the Great. *Dialogues*. New York: Catholic University Press, 1959.

Gutierrez, Gustavo. *We Drink from Our Own Wells: The Spiritual Journey of a People*. Maryknoll, NY: Orbis, 1998.

Gutierrez Aguilar, Raquel. *Rhythms of the Pachakuti: Indigenous Uprising and State Power in Bolivia*. Durham, NC: Duke University Press, 2014.

Hall, Amy Laura. *Conceiving Parenthood: American Protestantism and the Spirit of Reproduction*. Grand Rapids: Eerdmans, 2008.

Haraway, Donna. *Staying with the Trouble: Making Kin in the Chthulucene*. Durham, NC: Duke University Press, 2016.

Harris, Melanie. *Ecowomanism: African American Women and Earth-Honoring Faiths*. Maryknoll, NY: Orbis, 2017.

Harvey, Jennifer. *Raising White Kids: Bringing Up Children in a Racially Unjust America*. Nashville: Abingdon, 2017.

Hawken, Paul, ed. *Drawdown: The Most Comprehensive Plan Ever Proposed to Reverse Global Warming*. New York: Penguin, 2017.

Hebblethwaite, Margaret, and Peter Kavanagh. *Our Two Gardens*. Nashville: Oliver-Nelson, 1991.

Herbert, George. "The Twenty-Third Psalm." In *The Complete English Poems*, edited by John Tobin, 162–63. New York: Penguin, 2004.

Hollywood, Amy. "Song, Experience, and the Book in Benedictine Monasticism." In *Cambridge Companion to Christian Mysticism*, edited by Amy Hollywood and Patricia Z. Beckman, 59–79. New York: Cambridge University Press, 2012.

Holman, Susan. *The Hungry Are Dying: Beggars and Bishops in Roman Cappadocia*. New York: Oxford University Press, 2001.

Hossfeld, Frank-Lothar, and Erich Zenger. *Psalms 2: A Commentary on Psalms 51–100*. Minneapolis: Fortress, 2005.

———. *Psalms 3: A Commentary on Psalms 101–150*. Minneapolis: Fortress, 2001.

Huber, Matthew. *Climate Change as Class War: Building Socialism on a Warming Planet*. New York: Verso, 2022.

Illouz, Eva. *Cold Intimacies: The Making of Emotional Capitalism*. Malden, MA: Polity, 2007.

Bibliography

———. *Saving the Modern Soul: Therapy, Emotions, and the Culture of Self-Help*. Berkeley: University of California Press.

Isasi-Diaz, Ada Maria. "*Identifacate con Nostras*: A *Mujerista* Christological Understanding." In *Jesus in the Hispanic Community: Images of Christ from Theology to Popular Culture*, edited by Harold Recinos and Hugo Magallanes, 38–57. Louisville: Westminster John Knox, 2009.

———. "Mujerista Discourse: A Platform for Latinas' Subjugated Knowledge." In *Decolonizing Epistemologies: Latina/o Theology and Philosophy*, edited by Ada Maria Isasi-Diaz and Eduardo Mendieta, 44–67. New York: Fordham University Press, 2012.

———. *Mujerista Theology: A Theology for the Twenty-First Century*. Maryknoll, NY: Orbis, 1996.

Jantzen, Grace. *A Place of Springs: Death and the Displacement of Beauty*. Vol. 3. New York: Routledge, 2009.

Jerome. *The Homilies of Saint Jerome*, 1–59. Vol. 1, *On the Psalms*. Translated by Marie Liguori Ewald. Washington, DC: Catholic University Press, 1964.

———. "Letter XLVI." In *The Nicene and Post-Nicene Fathers*, vol. 6, *Saint Jerome: Letters and Select Works*, edited by Philip Schaff and Henry Wace, 60–65. New York: Christian Literature Company, 1893.

Joh, Wonhee Anne. "Relating to Household Labor Justly." In *Justice in a Global Economy: Strategies for Home, Community, and World*, edited by Pamela Brubaker et al., 29–39. Louisville: Westminster John Knox, 2006.

Jones, Serene. *Trauma and Grace: Theology in a Ruptured World*. Louisville: Westminster John Knox, 2009.

Katongole, Emmanuel. *Born from Lament: The Theology and Politics of Hope in Africa*. Grand Rapids: Eerdmans, 2017.

Katz, Cindi. "Childhood as Spectacle: Relays of Anxiety and the Reconfiguration of the Child." *Cultural Geographies* 15.1 (2008) 5–17.

———. *Growing Up Global: Economic Restructuring and Children's Everyday Lives*. Minneapolis: University of Minnesota Press, 2004.

———. "Just Managing: American Middle-Class Parenthood in Insecure Times." In *The Global Middle Classes: Theorizing Through Ethnography*, edited by R. Heiman et al., 169–86. Santa Fe: SAR, 2012.

Kaufman, Mark. "The Carbon Footprint Sham: A 'Successful, Deceptive' PR Campaign." *Mashable* July, 13, 2020. https://in.mashable.com/science/15520/the-carbon-footprint-sham.

Keller, Catherine. "The Becoming of Theopoetics: A Brief, Incongruent History." In *Intercarnations: Exercises in Theological Possibility*, 105–18. New York: Fordham University Press, 2017.

Kim, Soeng Lee. *Mark, Women, and Empire: A Korean Postcolonial Perspective*. Sheffield: Sheffield Phoenix, 2010.

Klein, Naomi. *This Changes Everything: Capitalism vs The Climate*. New York: Simon & Schuster, 2014.

Klinenberg, Eric. *Palaces for the People: How Social Infrastructure Can Help Fight Inequality, Polarization, and the Decline of Civic Life*. New York: Crown, 2018.

Knowles, Melody. "A Woman at Prayer: A Critical Note on Psalm 131:2b." *Journal of Biblical Literature* 125.2 (2006) 385–89.

Krause, Hans-Joachim. *Psalms 60–150*. Minneapolis: Augsburg Fortress, 1989.

Bibliography

Leclercq, Jean. *The Love of Learning and the Desire for God: A Study of Monastic Culture.* New York: Fordham University Press, 1982.

Lederach, John Paul. *The Moral Imagination: The Art and Soul of Building Peace.* New York: Oxford University Press, 2005.

Lee, Hak Joon. *God and Community Organizing: A Covenantal Approach.* Waco, TX: Baylor University Press, 2020.

Lewis, Stephen, et al. *Another Way: Living and Leading Change on Purpose.* St. Louis: Chalice, 2020.

Lohfink, Norbert, and Erich Zenger. *The God of Israel and the Nations: Studies in Isaiah and the Psalms.* Collegeville, MN: Liturgical, 2000.

Luther, Martin. *The Four Psalms of Comfort.* In *Luther's Works: Selected Psalms III*, vol. 14, edited by Jaroslav Pelikan. St. Louis: Concordia, 1958.

———. *The Seven Penitential Psalms.* In *Luther's Works: Selected Psalms III*, vol. 14, edited by Jaroslav Pelikan. St. Louis: Concordia, 1958.

Martell-Otero, Loida. "Of Satos and Saints: Salvation from the Periphery." *Perspectivas* 4 (2001) 7–38.

Mays, James. "Worship, World, and Power: An Interpretation of Psalm 100." *Interpretation* 23.3 (1969) 315–30.

McFague, Sallie. *Models of God: Theology for an Ecological, Nuclear Age.* Philadelphia: Fortress, 1987.

McLaren, Brian. *Finding Our Way Again: The Return of the Ancient Practices.* Nashville: Thomas Nelson, 2008.

McNeil, John. *A History of the Cure of Souls.* New York: Harper, 1951.

Miller, Patrick. *Interpreting the Psalms.* Philadelphia: Fortress, 1986.

Miller, Tina. *Making Sense of Fatherhood: Gender, Caring, and Work.* New York: Cambridge University Press, 2011.

Miller-McLemore, Bonnie. *Also a Mother: Work and Family as Theological Dilemma.* Nashville: Abingdon, 1994.

———. "Children and Religion in the Public Square: 'Too Dangerous and Too Safe, Too Difficult and Too Silly.'" *Journal of Religion* 86.3 (2006) 385–401.

———. *In the Midst of Chaos: Caring for Children as Spiritual Practice.* San Francisco: Josey-Bass, 2007.

Miranda, Jose. *Communism in the Bible.* Maryknoll, NY: Orbis, 1982.

Myers, Ched, ed. *Watershed Discipleship: Reinhabiting Bioregional Faith and Practice.* Eugene, OR: Cascade, 2016.

Nabhan, Gary Paul. *Jesus for Farmers and Fishers: Justice for All Those Marginalized by Our Food System.* Minneapolis: Broadleaf, 2021.

Nabhan, Gary Paul, and Stephen Trimble. *The Geography of Childhood: Why Children Need Wild Places.* Boston: Beacon, 1994.

Nagara, Innosanto. *A is for Activist.* New York: Seven Stories, 2013.

Nanko-Fernandez, Carmen. "*Lo Cotindiano* as *Locus Theologicus.*" In *The Wiley Blackwell Companion to Latino/a Theology*, edited by Orlando Espin, 15–33. Camden, NJ: Wiley-Blackwell, 2015.

Norgaard, Kari Marie. *Living in Denial: Climate Change, Emotions, and Everyday Life.* Cambridge: MIT Press, 2011.

Norris, Kathleen. *Amazing Grace: A Vocabulary of Grace.* New York: Riverhead, 1998.

Oduyoye, Mercy Amba. *Introducing African Women's Theology.* Sheffield: Sheffield Academic, 2001.

Bibliography

Oh, Jea Sophia. "Salim, Women, and Oikos: A Planetary Expansion of Family." In *Valuing Lives, Healing Earth*, edited by Lilian Dube et al., 47–56. Louvain: Peeters, 2021.

Parish, Nurya Love. *Resurrection Matters: Church Renewal for Creation's Sake*. New York: Church, 2018.

Patel, Raj, and Jason Moore. *A History of the World in Seven Cheap Things: A Guide to Capitalism, Nature, and the Future of the Planet*. Oakland, CA: University of California Press, 2017.

Peterson, Anna. *Everyday Ethics and Social Change: The Education of Desire*. New York: Columbia University Press, 2009.

Quintana, Laura. *The Politics of Bodies: Philosophical Emancipation with and beyond Ranciere*. New York: Rowman & Littlefield, 2020.

Randall, Margaret. *Christians in the Nicaraguan Revolution*. Vancouver: New Star, 1983.

Rashi. *Rashi's Commentary on Psalms*. Leiden: Brill, 2004.

Reid, Stephen. "David and the Political Theology of the Psalter." In *The Psalter as Witness: Theology, Poetry, and Genre*, edited by Dennis Tucker and W. H. Bellinger, 47–62. Waco, TX: Baylor University Press, 2017.

———. *Listening In: A Multicultural Reading of the Psalms*. Nashville: Abingdon, 1997.

Rieger, Joerg. *Christ and Empire: From Paul to Postcolonial Times*. Minneapolis: Fortress, 2007.

———. *No Rising Tide: Theology, Economics, and the Future*. Minneapolis: Fortress, 2009.

———. *Theology in the Capitalocene: Ecology, Identity, Class, and Solidarity*. Minneapolis: Fortress, 2022.

Rieger, Joerg, and Kwok, Pui-lan. *Occupy Religion: Theology of the Multitude*. New York: Rowman & Littlefield, 2012.

Rieger, Joerg, and Rosemarie Henkel-Rieger. *United We Are a Force: How Faith and Labor Can Overcome America's Inequalities*. St. Louis: Chalice, 2016.

Rogers-Vaughn, Bruce. *Caring for Souls in a Neoliberal Age*. New York: Palgrave Macmillan, 2016.

Rowson, Jonathan. *A New Agenda on Climate Change: Facing up to Stealth Denial and Winding Down on Fossil Fuels*. London: Royal Society of Arts, 2013.

Ruether, Rosemary Radford. *New Woman/New Earth: Sexist Ideologies and Human Liberation*. New York: Seabury, 1975.

———. *Gaia and God: An Ecofeminist Theology of Earth Healing*. San Francisco: Harper, 1996.

Ryan-Simpkins, Kelsey, and Nogueira-Godsey, Elaine. "Tangible Actions Toward Solidarity: An Ecofeminist Analysis of Women's Participation in Food Justice." In *Valuing Lives, Healing Earth*, edited by Lilian Dube et al., 203–22. Louvain: Peeters, 2021.

Saad, Lydia, and Jeffrey M. Jones. "U.S. Concern about Global Warming at Eight-Year High." *Gallup*, March 16, 2016. http://www.gallup.com/poll/190010/concernglobal-warming-eightyear-high.aspx.

Salvatierra, Alexia, and Peter Heltzel. *Faith-Rooted Organizing: Mobilizing the Church in Service to the World*. Downers Grove, IL: InterVarsity, 2014.

Saverin, Diana. "The Thoreau of the Suburbs." *The Atlantic*, February 5, 2015. https://www.theatlantic.com/culture/archive/2015/02/the-thoreau-of-the-suburbs/385128/.

Schade, Leah, and Margaret Bullitt-Jonas, eds. *Rooted and Rising: Voices of Courage in a Time of Climate Crisis*. New York: Rowman & Littlefield, 2019.

Schaefer, Konrad. *Psalms*. Collegeville, MN: Liturgical, 2001.

Bibliography

Shove, Elizabeth. *Comfort, Cleanliness, and Convivence: The Social Organization of Normality*. New York: Berg, 2003.

Simmons, Walter. *Cities of Ladies: Beguine Communities in the Medieval Low Countries, 1200–1565*. Philadelphia: University of Pennsylvania Press, 2003.

Soelle, Dorothee. *Suffering*. Philadelphia: Fortress, 1975.

Steussy, Marti. *Psalms*. St. Louis: Chalice, 2004.

Thatamanil, John. "Constructive Theology as Theopoetics: Theological Construction as Divine-Human Creativity." In *What is Constructive Theology?: Histories, Methodologies, and Perspectives*, edited by Marion Grau and Jason Wyman, 31–52. New York: T&T Clark, 2020.

Townes, Emilie. *Breaking the Fine Rain of Death: African American Health Issues and a Womanist Ethic of Care*. New York: Continuum, 2001.

———. *In a Blaze of Glory: Womanist Spirituality as Social Witness*. Nashville: Abingdon, 1995.

———. *Womanist Ethics and the Cultural Production of Evil*. New York: Palgrave Macmillan, 2006.

Tran, Jonathan. *Foucault and Theology*. New York: T&T Clark, 2011.

———. "The Otherness of Children as a Hint of an Outside: Michel Foucault, Richard Yates and Karl Barth on Suburban Life." *Theology and Sexuality*. 15.2 (2009) 191–211.

Vanderslice, Kendall. *We Will Feast: Rethinking Dinner, Worship, and the Community of God*. Grand Rapids: Eerdmans, 2019.

Vest, Norvene. *No Moment Too Small: Rhythms of Silence, Prayer, and Holy Reading*. Kalamazoo, MI: Cistercian, 1994.

Walker-Jones, Arthur. *The Green Psalter: Resources for an Ecological Spirituality*. Minneapolis: Fortress, 2009.

Wall, John. *Ethics in Light of Childhood*. Washington, DC: Georgetown University Press, 2010.

Walsh, Catherine. "The Decolonial *For*: Resurgences, Shifts, and Movements." In *On Decoloniality: Concepts, Analytics, Praxis*, 15–32. Durham, NC: Duke University Press, 2018.

Weeks, Kathi. *The Problem with Work: Feminism, Marxism, Antiwork Politics, and Postwork Imaginaries*. Durham, NC: Duke University Press, 2011.

Weintrobe, Sally. "The Difficult Problem of Thinking about Anxiety with Climate Change." In *Engaging with Climate Change: Psychoanalytic and Interdisciplinary Perspectives*, edited by Sally Weintrobe, 33–37. New York: Routledge, 2013.

West, Mona. "Queer *Lectio Divina*." In *Queering Christianity: Finding a Place at the Table for LGBTQI Christians*, edited by Robert Shore-God et al., 371–79. Santa Barbara, CA: Praeger, 2013, 371–379.

Winant, Gabriel. *The Next Shift: The Fall of Industry and the Rise of Health Care in Rust Belt America*. Cambridge: Harvard University Press, 2021.

Wirzba, Norman. *Food and Faith: A Theology of Eating*. New York: Cambridge University Press, 2011.

Woofenden, Anna. *This is God's Table: Finding Church Beyond the Walls*. Harrisonburg, PA: Herald, 2020.

Wylie-Kellerman, Lydia, ed. *Sandbox Revolution: Raising Kids for a Just World*. Minneapolis: Broadleaf, 2021.

Zibechi, Raul. *Dispersing Power: Social Movements as Anti-State Forces*. Oakland, CA: AK, 2010.

Made in the USA
Columbia, SC
01 June 2024

36490128R00098